9/00

THE NAZI O   S

D1190916

H.R. 10.0

Pts. 3.0

THE NAZI OLYMPICS
BERLIN 1936

SUSAN D. BACHRACH
UNITED STATES HOLOCAUST MEMORIAL MUSEUM

 LITTLE, BROWN AND COMPANY

BOSTON NEW YORK LONDON

ALSO BY SUSAN D. BACHRACH

Tell Them We Remember: The Story of the Holocaust

Copyright © 2000 by the United States Holocaust Memorial Council

First Edition
Book design: Lisa Diercks
Typeset in Scala (FontShop)

Library of Congress Cataloging-in-Publication Data

Bachrach, Susan D.
    The Nazi Olympics : Berlin 1936 / by Susan D. Bachrach.—1st ed.
        p. cm.
    Includes bibliographical references and index.
    Summary: Recounts the story of the Olympics held in Berlin in 1936, and how the Nazis attempted to turn the games into a propaganda tool for their cause.
    ISBN 0-316-07086-6 (hc)
    ISBN 0-316-07087-4 (pb)
    1. Olympic Games (11th : 1936 : Berlin, Germany) Juvenile literature.
2. Olympics—Political aspects—Germany—History—1933–1945 Juvenile literature. [1. Olympic Games (11th : 1936 : Berlin, Germany)] I. Title.
GV722 1936.B27 2000
796.48—dc21   99-31423

10 9 8 7 6 5 4 3 2 1

MV-NY

Printed in the United States of America

CONTENTS

PART ONE

1933-1936: NAZI GERMANY

PART TWO

THE NAZIFICATION OF GERMAN SPORT

PART THREE

THE BOYCOTT DEBATE

ACKNOWLEDGMENTS

This book is based on the special exhibition *Nazi Olympics: Berlin 1936,* which opened at the United States Holocaust Memorial Museum in July 1996, on the occasion of the sixtieth anniversary of the 1936 Olympic Games and the opening of the 1996 Summer Olympics in Atlanta. Many members of the museum program and support divisions contributed to the exhibition, and it would not have been possible without all their efforts. As reflected in the photo credits for this book, the exhibition drew on the resources of many institutions and individual collectors across the country and abroad.

The museum's core team for the exhibition was led by Sara J. Bloomfield and Stephen Goodell and included Gail Kaplan Fishman, Greg Naranjo, Alice Greenwald, Jonathan Friedman, Daniel Greene, Jonathan Roos, Derek Symer, Andrew Campagna, Clare Cronin, Nancy Gillette, Elizabeth Laitman, Ernest Latham, Ted Phillips, and Karen Wyatt. Ed Owen was the photographer, and Lauriston Marshall worked with the exhibition designers, Point Zero of Los Angeles. Academic advisers for the exhibition were Gary Allison, George Eisen, James Gilbert, John Hoberman, Deborah Lipstadt, Richard Mandel, Sybil Milton, Jeffrey Sammons, and David Wiggins. The late Randy Goldman conducted interviews of former athletes for a video production by Hillmann & Carr of Washington, D.C.

Several museum colleagues provided special help on this book: Paul Rose, Satu Haase-Webb, Carrie Feld, Dina Danon, Linda Bixby, Sharon Muller, Judy Cohen, Leslie Swift, Linda Melone, and Paul Thomas. The chronology for the book draws on teaching materials developed for the traveling exhibition *Nazi Olympics* by David Klevan of the museum's education staff, led by Joan Ringelheim. At Little,

Brown, John G. Keller, vice president and publisher of children's books, directed the project, and his assistant, Leila Little, and Senior Copyeditor Pamela Marshall worked on the book. Lisa Diercks was the designer.

A great pleasure for those of us working on this exhibition was meeting some of the athletes whose stories the museum told. It was a privilege to speak to former Olympians John Woodruff, Marty Glickman, and Herman Goldberg. Milton Greene and Leo Merson helped us understand the perspective of athletes who boycotted the Olympic trials, and Margaret Lambert provided us with insights into her experiences as a star high jumper denied the opportunity to compete in Nazi Germany.

The subject of this exhibition was a serious one, the use of the Olympics by the Nazi regime for the purposes of propaganda. Part of the work, however, required delving into sports history. At home, I have enjoyed talking about this topic with my husband, Peter, and our athletic children, Annie and Ben. At work, I have had the pleasure of discussing track and field with the museum's knowledgeable director of exhibitions, Steve Goodell. This book is for all sports aficionados like them interested in understanding the political and social backdrop of the 1936 Games.

PRELUDE: **BERLIN IS CHOSEN TO HOST THE 1936 OLYMPICS**

On May 13, 1931, the president of the International Olympic Committee (IOC), Belgian Count Henri de Baillet-Latour, announced that Berlin, the capital of Germany, would be the site of the 1936 Summer Olympics. The selection was made by a mail ballot of committee members, with forty-three votes for Berlin and sixteen for Barcelona, Spain. The choice was made more than five years in advance of the Olympics to give the host city enough time to prepare for the event.

In 1931 the modern Olympics movement was still in its childhood. Reviving the Olympic Games first held in ancient Greece was the idea of a French citizen, Baron Pierre de Coubertin. He saw the Olympics as a way to promote goodwill among nations. The first modern Olympiad was held in Athens, Greece, in 1896. A total of 245 male athletes from 14 nations competed in 43 events.

In the forty years between 1896 and 1936, the Games did not

Count Henri de Baillet-Latour (1876–1942) was typical of the many International Olympic Committee members, born into privilege and conservative in outlook. A childhood friend of the future king of Belgium, Albert I, Baillet-Latour was a diplomat and fervent horseman. In 1903 his social contacts won him membership in the IOC as did his wealth—in an era when IOC members not only paid their own travel expenses but also contributed to the costs of the organization. In 1925, Baillet-Latour succeeded Baron Pierre de Coubertin as IOC president, a position he held until his death.

Two Jews were among Germany's earliest Olympic medalists. Felix Gustav Flatow (*standing, first from left*) and Alfred Flatow (*middle row, second from right*) won first-place medals in gymnastics at the Athens Games in 1896. The two men were cousins. *Forum für Sportgeschichte— Förderverein für das Sport-museum Berlin, Collection of Stefan Flatow.*

enjoy steady growth, and at times it seemed as if Coubertin's creation might not survive. With the exception of Athens's ten-day sports festival, until 1932 the length of the competition for all the Games was weeks or even months (see Appendix 1).

From the beginning of the modern Olympics, events outside the world of sport affected the Games. World War I (1914–1918) forced the cancellation of the 1916 Games scheduled for Berlin. The war embittered relations among enemy nations for many years thereafter. Games were held in Antwerp, Belgium, in 1920, but the host country did not invite any teams from Germany or its allies that had fought against Belgians during the war. When Paris hosted the Olympics in 1924, France did not invite Germany to send a team. It was only at Amsterdam in 1928, ten years after the end of the war, that Germans were again invited to the Olympics. The team did well, winning the second highest number of medals, trailing only the United States.

In the 1932 Games in Los Angeles many athletes could not compete because of the worldwide economic depression and the high cost of traveling to the city from Europe. Participation was the lowest since 1906. Only 1,408 athletes competed, compared to 3,014 in the 1928 Olympics. Germany did not send a large team to California and finished only ninth in the total medal count.

When the International Olympic Committee awarded Berlin the 1936 Summer Olympics in 1931, the choice was another sign of Germany's being included once more in the world community.

University of Michigan track star William DeHart Hubbard became the first African American to win an individual gold medal in track and field. In Paris in 1924 he jumped 24 feet 5 inches in the long jump. In 1936 Jesse Owens would better this mark by 2 feet. *UPI/Corbis-Bettmann, New York, N.Y.*

Dr. Theodor Lewald (1860–1947) was seventy-one years old in 1931 when the International Olympic Committee chose Berlin to host the 1936 Games. A career civil servant, he had performed such duties as representing Germany at world's fairs and administering the finances for early German Olympic teams. Lewald was president of the German Olympic Committee from 1919 to 1934. He became a member of the International Olympic Committee in 1926, when he was chairman of the Committee for Physical Exercise, an umbrella organization for German sports. *Cigaretten-Bilderdienst GmbH, Die Olympischen Spiele 1936: in Berlin und Garmisch-Partenkirchen (Hamburg-Bahrenfeld, 1936).*

Carl Diem (1882–1962) accompanied the German Olympic team to Athens in 1906 and served as captain of the German team at the 1912 Stockholm Games. From 1913 to 1916 he was general secretary of the 1916 Berlin Games. Diem and Lewald worked as a team planning the 1936 Olympics. It was Diem who created the idea of a relay of Olympic torch runners, modeled on a torch run that occurred in Athens in 80 B.C. Diem survived World War II, and in 1951 he became a member of the new Federal Republic of Germany's Olympic committee. He is considered one of the greatest sports historians of the twentieth century. *UPI/Corbis-Bettmann, New York, N.Y.*

The selection of Berlin also showed the international Olympic community's respect for two German sports leaders, Dr. Theodor Lewald and Carl Diem. Both men had been involved in plans for the 1916 Berlin Games that were canceled. For years they had been urging their friends in the Olympics movement to let them bring the Games back to Germany. Lewald and Diem were both very pleased when they were granted their wish and set to the task of planning the Berlin Games, an event they had been dreaming about for more than fifteen years.

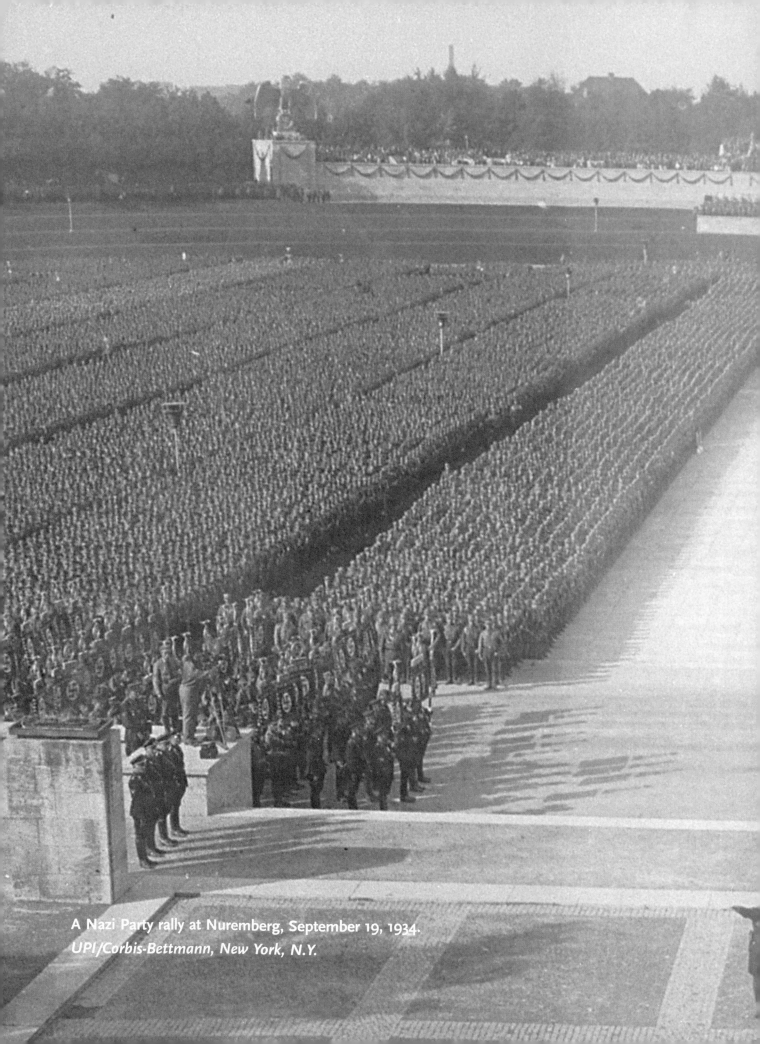

A Nazi Party rally at Nuremberg, September 19, 1934.
UPI/Corbis-Bettmann, New York, N.Y.

PART ONE

1933–1936: NAZI GERMANY

HITLER COMES TO POWER

Two years after the International Olympic Committee chose Berlin as the site for the 1936 Summer Olympics, a major political change took place in Germany that neither its members nor German Olympic organizers Dr. Theodor Lewald and Carl Diem had expected. On January 30, 1933, the German president, Paul von Hindenburg, appointed Adolf Hitler chancellor, the head of the government.

Hitler was the leader of an extreme right-wing political party, the National Socialist German Workers (Nazi) Party. In the early 1930s the Nazis won growing support among Germans at a time of high unemployment, hunger, business failures, and great political and social unrest. Hitler and the Nazis promised the birth of a "new Germany," giving hope to many Germans fearful of the future.

In their appeals to German citizens, the Nazis said that a "new Germany" would have different boundaries. Their aim was to make German-speaking peoples living in Austria and other neighboring

German chancellor and Nazi Party leader Adolf Hitler reviews thirty-five thousand storm troopers, members of the Nazi Party's paramilitary wing called the SA (*Sturmabteilung*), February 20, 1936. *USHMM Photo Archives.*

countries part of one German community and to gain more land for this united Germanic population by conquering eastern Europe.

To win back Austria and other territories that had been part of the large Austrian-German empire before World War I and to expand well beyond them, Hitler needed to rebuild Germany's military strength. After he took power, government funding for the purchase of tanks, airplanes, and other weapons rose steadily. A stronger military also required more and better-trained soldiers. In 1935 Hitler's government issued a law requiring all young men to serve one year in the German armed forces.

The re-arming of Germany took place despite terms of the Treaty of Versailles of 1919, which Germany had signed. This treaty that ended World War I had aimed to prevent Germany from again becoming a major military power and threat.

THE POLICE STATE

J ust as Hitler refused to respect terms of the Treaty of Versailles, he also did not intend to govern Germany as a democratic leader. Under the first two months of his rule, the German parliament took away German citizens' freedoms of speech, assembly, and the press and other rights. Police could enter homes without a search warrant, listen in on telephone conversations, and intercept mail. The parliament also passed the "Enabling Act," which gave Hitler the power to establish a dictatorship.

Armed storm troopers dressed in Nazi uniforms and black leather boots rounded up thousands of men and women who opposed Hitler's rule, including liberals, Socialists, Communists, trade unionists, and writers. The Nazis held thousands of political opponents without trial in prisons. To make room for the overflow of prisoners, in March 1933, a large concentration camp was opened at Dachau, a small town near the city of Munich in southern Germany, and many others were built elsewhere.

Storm troopers round up political opponents of the Nazi regime, 1933. *Bildarchiv Preussischer Kulturbesitz, Berlin, Germany.*

Inmates perform forced labor at Dachau, the first Nazi concentration camp. *Bundesarchiv Koblenz, Germany.*

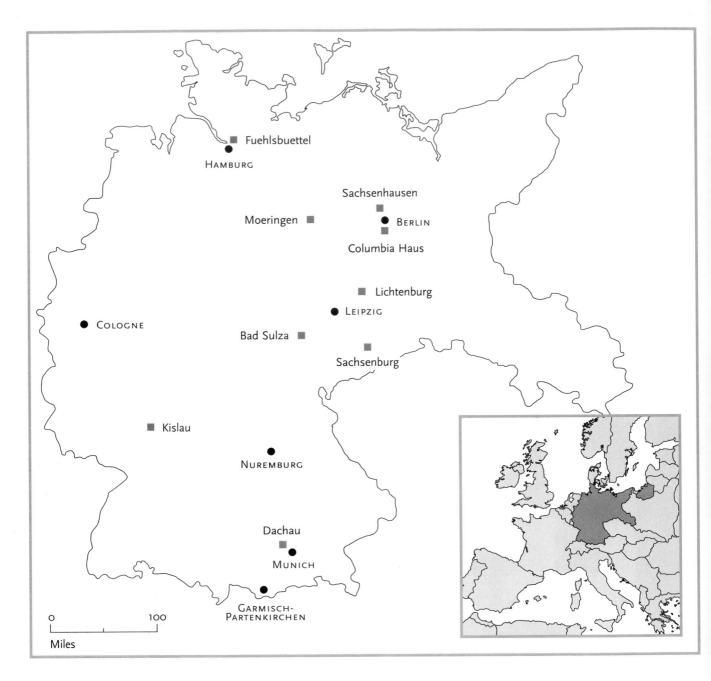

Concentration camps in Germany, 1936. *USHMM.*

Conditions in the concentration camps were cruel, as hard labor, strict discipline, and beatings were the rule. Prisoners lived in poorly heated and poorly ventilated wooden barracks and were fed starvation rations. The camps were meant to punish Nazi "enemies" and to scare all Germans into obedience. Many people fled Germany to neighboring countries to escape the Nazi terror.

NAZI RACISM AND ANTISEMITISM

In speeches Hitler spoke often about the importance of "racial purity" and the superiority of the "Germanic race"—the so-called Aryan master race. The Nazis spread their racist beliefs in classrooms and through books, newspapers, movies, radio, and posters. In the "new Germany" there was no place for "non-Aryans," considered racial inferiors.

Jews made up the largest minority group in Germany. In 1933 one-half million Jews, most of whom thought of themselves as Germans, were defined by the Nazis as "non-Aryans" and faced new forms of discrimination. Tens of thousands of others who were not Jewish but had close relatives—a parent or grandparent—who had been raised Jewish also became victims of Nazi racial policies because they, too, were considered "non-Aryans." It did not matter whether or not they viewed themselves as Jews, worshiped in a synagogue, or in any way followed Jewish religious beliefs.

The lives of Jewish men, women, and children changed dramat-

In Nazi Germany, public schoolteachers gave classes in "racial hygiene" that claimed the superiority of the "Aryan race." In this illustration from the Nazi magazine *Neues Volk* (New People), elementary school students listen as their teacher compares the physical characteristics of one of their classmates to racial "types" as classified on widely used charts, 1934. *USHMM Photo Archives.*

ically in Nazi Germany. They went from being accepted members of German society to outcasts, segregated from non-Jews. In the early 1930s—the years before foreign visitors flocked to Berlin for the 1936 Olympics—the Nazi campaign against Jews, like the Nazi terror against political enemies, was reported in newspapers in the United States and other western nations. Readers learned about Nazi storm troopers' physical attacks on Jews, the Nazi-organized boycott of Jewish businesses, the dismissal of Jews from the law and medical professions and from teaching and other civil service positions, and the barring of Jews from movie theaters, parks, and other places of recreation. Stories appeared on the burning of books by Jewish authors and new laws that limited the number of Jewish students who could attend public schools and universities.

Foreign journalists also reported on the announcement of anti-Jewish laws at a Nazi Party rally held in the city of Nuremberg in September 1935. The "Nuremberg Laws" prohibited Jews from marrying or having sexual relations with "persons of German or related blood." Viewed as having "alien blood" that placed them outside the national community, Jews were no longer allowed to display the German flag. When the new military law went into effect in October 1935, Jewish men were not called up to serve in the army because after Nuremberg they were no longer considered full-fledged German citizens.

Hateful propaganda scapegoated Jews, unfairly blaming them for all of Germany's problems. In towns and cities all over Germany, local leaders posted signs announcing that Jews were not welcome. As a result, many Jews moved from smaller towns into large cities such as Berlin, where their identity was less easily known. Many other Jews left Germany to live in neighboring France, the Netherlands, Czechoslovakia, or elsewhere.

The sign says, "Jews not wanted in Tölz!," 1935. UPI/Corbis-Bettmann, New York, N.Y.

Other groups in Germany also suffered during the Nazi drive to create a strong, pure "Aryan master race." On July 14, 1933, a law was proclaimed that aimed to strengthen the "Aryan" population by weeding out "bad" genes from the total German gene pool. This law mandated the sterilization of persons suffering from mental and physical diseases or conditions thought to be inherited, such as "feeble-mindedness," schizophrenia, epilepsy, blindness, and deafness. By preventing such individuals from having children, the Nazis believed that Germany could greatly reduce the number of "unhealthy" families in future generations. Physicians and judges who served on special "hereditary health courts" selected as many as four hundred thousand men and women, most between the ages of twenty and forty, to undergo operations that made them sterile.

Most victims of the forced sterilizations were "Aryan" Germans. But the policy was also used against some "non-Aryans."

LEFT: "Jews are unwelcome in Heisede," 1935. *Archives of the YIVO Institute for Jewish Research, New York, N.Y.*

RIGHT: "Jews unwelcome in Hildesheim," 1935. *Stadtarchiv Nürnberg, Germany.*

A slide for a lecture on genetics and race at the State Academy for Race and Health in Dresden, Germany, focuses on one of the five hundred children in Germany referred to as "Rhineland bastards" and viewed by the Nazis as racially inferior to their Germanic classmates, c. 1936. *Library of Congress, Washington, D.C.*

Germany had a very small black population, consisting mainly of five hundred teenagers widely referred to as the "Rhineland bastards." These children's mothers were Germans and their fathers were African soldiers, members of French colonial troops stationed in the Rhineland, in southwestern Germany, in the years after World War I.

An unknown number of Gypsies were also sterilized against their will. Nearly twenty thousand Gypsies, members of the Sinti and Roma tribes, lived in Germany in 1933. Like the "Rhineland bastards," Gypsies were treated as social outcasts long before Hitler came to power. *Zigeuner,* the German word for Gypsy, derives from a Greek root meaning "untouchable." Many Gypsies' darker skin color and traditional way of life, which included moving from place to place, set them apart from the rest of the population.

Thousands of girls execute a rhythmic calisthenics drill during a Nazi Party sporting event at Nuremberg, 1934. *UPI/Corbis-Bettmann, New York, N.Y.*

PART TWO
THE NAZIFICATION OF GERMAN SPORT

NAZI SPORT

In Nazi Germany all areas of public life—government, the military, education, the arts, and newspapers, radio, and other media—were brought into line with Nazi ideals and policies, or nazified. Even German sport did not escape this process of nazification. Hitler's government used sport in its drive to "purify" and strengthen the "Aryan race" and to prepare German youth for war. Nazi sport stressed the health and strength of the entire community over any one individual's athletic achievements. Images of German athletes spread the myth of "Aryan" racial superiority and physical power. Artists drew athletes with well-developed muscles and heroic strength and emphasized the "ideal Aryan" facial features—blue eyes and blond hair.

Such images also showed the great importance that Nazi leaders placed on physical fitness and education. Hitler reportedly said, "I want my youth strong and beautiful. I will train them in all of the athletic sciences. I want an athletic youth. That's the first and most

The magazine *Das Deutsche Mädel* (The German Girl) portrays the "ideal" female Aryan athlete, August 1935. *John Loaring.*

important thing." In 1936 the time devoted to physical education in schools went from two to three hours per week, and in 1938, to five hours. Cross-country running, soccer, and boxing were added to the curriculum because the Nazis believed that these sports promoted a spirit of attack and physical superiority. The comments that physical education teachers made on report cards became more important than those made by teachers of mathematics, science, and other academic subjects. Poor performance in sports could result in a student's being expelled from school.

Outside of school, Nazi youth groups used sports and hiking to bring boys and girls into one national community. Nazi sport prepared boys for war and girls to become physically fit mothers.

Volk und Raffe

September 1936   Heft 9

The motto of Hitler Youth was "*Fuehrer* [leader], command—we follow!" Hitler Youth members marched in drills, pitched tents in straight lines, played military games, and sang songs with such titles as "Soldiers Carry Rifles." By 1939, nearly nine million boys and girls belonged to Nazi youth groups for children ten years and older.

Older members of the Hitler Youth throw mock hand grenades ("potato mashers") during a sports festival, June 1936. *Ullstein Bilderdienst, Berlin, Germany.*

German police perform calisthenics in Berlin's Sport Palace, later the site of the Olympic handball competition, 1936. *FPG International, New York, N.Y.*

THE NAZI TAKEOVER OF THE OLYMPICS

When Hitler came to power in 1933, the German Olympic Committee's president, Dr. Theodor Lewald, and its secretary, Carl Diem, feared that Hitler would cancel plans for Germany to host the 1936 Olympics. The ideas about national power, military strength, and race that Hitler and other leading Nazis promoted seemed far from Olympic ideals of international goodwill. Indeed, before 1933, Nazi party spokesmen had not thought well of the Olympics. At the time of the 1932 Games in Los Angeles, one Nazi writer described the Games as an "infamous festival organized by Jews."

At first Hitler also held the Olympics in low regard, but he became a strong supporter after Joseph Goebbels, his Minister of Propaganda, convinced him that the Games were an excellent opportunity to show the world the "new Germany." Hitler's government also viewed the Olympics as a chance to increase the flow of desired foreign monies into Germany. At a meeting with Lewald

Hitler inspects the Olympic stadium under construction in Berlin, fall 1934. *Süddeutscher Verlag Bilderdienst, Munich, Germany.*

in March 1933, Hitler assured him that he would support the Olympics. A few months later, Hitler also promised full financial support for the event, 20,000,000 Reichsmarks ($8,000,000), and approved the plans for an impressive new sports complex.

A Nazi close to Hitler, Hans von Tschammer und Osten, headed the Reich Sports Office. This government agency controlled all sports organizations and clubs in Germany. In 1934

Hans von Tschammer und Osten (1887–1943) joined the Nazi Party in 1929, became SA colonel in 1931, and was promoted to SA major general in 1932. In July 1933, Hitler appointed him Reich Sports Office leader. In this position Tschammer und Osten established a system of segregation in German sports that denied Jews and others viewed as "non-Aryans" the opportunity to compete. He supervised sports competitions for the Hitler Youth and the SA and developed a program incorporating military sports into the training of German teachers. *Cigaretten-Bilderdienst GmbH,* Die Olympischen Spiele 1936: in Berlin und Garmisch-Partenkirchen *(Hamburg-Bahrenfeld, 1936).*

Tschammer und Osten became president of the German Olympic Committee, which selected the athletes for the German team. He replaced Lewald, who was removed after some Nazis protested his "non-Aryan" background—a Jewish father.

Tschammer und Osten tried to bind athletes to the Nazi regime by setting up national training and political-education camps. In late 1934 athletes chosen as members of the core team for the 1936 Olympics participated in a special public ceremony broadcast on the radio. The athletes pledged allegiance to the guidelines developed by the Reich Sports Office and swore that they would be worthy representatives of Germany, the Fatherland, in the Games.

THE PERSECUTION OF JEWISH ATHLETES

I n April 1933 Tschammer und Osten's Reich Sports Office ordered an "Aryans only" policy in all German athletic organizations. "Non-Aryans"—Jewish or part Jewish and Gypsy athletes—were systematically excluded from German sports associations and from public pools, gymnasiums, and other sports facilities. They were allowed segregated, third-class training facilities, and their opportunities to compete were limited. On May 29, 1933, the *New York Times* reported Tschammer und Osten's message to the German nation about preparations for the 1936 Olympics: "German sports are for Aryans," he stated. "German youth leadership is only for Aryans and not for Jews."

Many athletes' careers were interrupted. Daniel Prenn, one of Germany's top-ranked tennis players and ranked number six in the world, was removed from Germany's Davis Cup team, as reported by the *New York Times* and other American newspapers. Like a number of athletes, Prenn moved to England, where he

RIGHT: Helene Mayer (1910–1953) was born in Offenbach, Germany, to a Christian mother and a Jewish father. Athletically gifted, she won the German foil championship at fourteen and three years later took the gold medal in the foil at the Amsterdam Olympics. She won the world championship in 1929 and 1931. At the 1932 Olympics at Los Angeles she finished only fifth because she was ill. Remaining in California to study law, she was shocked to learn of her expulsion in 1933 from the Offenbach Fencing Club. This effectively barred her from competing for the 1936 German Olympic team— even though she was considered the greatest woman fencer in the world, and with her striking blonde and tall appearance she looked like the Nazi ideal "Aryan" woman. *Dr. George Eisen.*

LEFT: Gretel Bergmann (1914–) grew up in a small town near Ulm, Germany. She had two brothers and developed her athletic talents by playing soccer and handball on boys' teams made up mostly of non-Jews. Her life as a German Jew was uneventful until 1933, when Hitler took power. Then non-Jewish friends could no longer meet with her publicly and had to sneak into her house at night to see her. One of her neighborhood friends acted as if they had never known each other. Bergmann wanted to pursue studies in physical education at Berlin University, but officials there withdrew her admission, telling her to wait until "everything blew over." In the fall of 1933, her father, a factory owner with contacts abroad, took her to England, where she enrolled in English studies and continued to train and compete. *Margaret (Gretel Bergmann) Lambert.*

Jewish tennis star Daniel Prenn played at Wimbledon in 1934 after he emigrated to England. But in his struggle to make a new life abroad, tennis would become less important to him. *The Wimbledon Lawn Tennis Museum, London, United Kingdom.*

played tennis. In April 1933 the German Boxing Federation expelled amateur champion Erich Seelig because he was Jewish. Seelig later resumed his boxing career in England, then emigrated to the United States. As American readers of the *Times* learned on November 24, 1933, fencer Helene Mayer, gold-medal winner for

The entrance to the public beach at the Wannsee section of Berlin bears the sign "Entrance to Jews Is Prohibited," 1935. *Roger et Viollet, Paris, France.*

The list is a sample of actions taken in Germany to bar Jews or "non-Aryans" from sports clubs and facilities in the three years before the 1936 Olympics.

March 1933 The city of Cologne bans Jews from city playgrounds and sports facilities.

April 4, 1933 The German Boxing Federation bans Jewish boxers from competitive bouts. All contracts arranged by Jewish fight promoters are to be canceled.

April 25, 1933 The Reich Sports Office orders all German gymnastic organizations to adopt an "Aryans only" policy. The order does not apply to Jewish war veterans or their descendants.

May 24, 1933 The German Gymnastic Society decrees that members of their organization must prove "Aryan" ancestry.

June 2, 1933 The Ministry of Science in the German state of Prussia orders that village, city, county, and district physical education organizations expel Jewish members.

July 9, 1933 The All-German Chess Convention excludes Jews from its membership.

August 22, 1933 No Jews are allowed to use public swimming pools in Wannsee (Berlin), Fulda, Beuthen, Speyer, and elsewhere.

September/October 1933 "Non-Aryans" cannot work as professional or amateur jockeys.

March 7, 1934 The Reich Youth Leadership announces that German Jewish youth groups cannot wear uniforms.

June 19, 1935 The Minister of Interior for the German state of Baden prohibits group hikes and similar activities for all non–National Socialist Party youth groups.

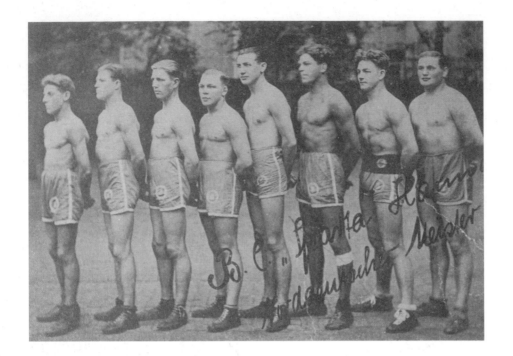

Sinti boxer Johann Trollmann (*third from right*) with his German workers' sports club, "Sparta" Hanover, a few years before German sports officials barred him from boxing, 1929. *Hans Firzlaff.*

World-class high jumper Gretel Bergmann (*second row, third from right*) with her track club in Ulm before she was expelled in the summer of 1933, c. 1929. *Margaret (Gretel Bergmann) Lambert.*

Denied the right to play on existing sports fields, Bergmann (*foreground, in black shirt*) and other members of her Jewish sports club prepare to transform a former potato patch into a handball field, 1933. *Margaret (Gretel Bergmann) Lambert.*

Germany in the 1928 Olympics, was expelled from her fencing club in Offenbach, Germany—even though Mayer was living in the United States at the time—because one of her parents was Jewish. Gypsies, including the Sinti boxer Johann Trollmann, were also purged from German sports. In June 1933, Trollman, the German middleweight boxing champion, was banned from boxing for "racial reasons."

Gretel Bergmann, a world-class high jumper, was expelled from her German sports club in Ulm in the summer of 1933 because she was Jewish. Bergmann trained briefly with a separate Jewish sports club in 1933. But Jewish sports facilities were no match for those of the well-funded German groups. Bergmann, like Prenn, went to England to compete, and she won the British women's high jump title in 1934.

1936 Olympics May Be Canceled Du

BERLIN FACES LOSS OF OLYMPIC GAMES

Anti-Semitic Attitude of Hitler Government May Cause Shift to Rome or Tokyo.

OFFICIALS HERE UNEASY

Brundage Doubts U. S. Would Be Represented if Jews Were Bar

TALK

Entire Qu
Internat
Meets

By A

Transfer
Olympic
Berlin in 1
a result
titude of th

This deve
a statemen
president o
Committee
YORK TIME
cago, and
dispatch fr
text of a le
to the edi
tion there.

Three

The poss
those resp
are:

First, th
may be c
Rome or Tokyo, the two named
have expressed an eagerness to
handle the Olympics should they be
taken away from Germany.

Second, the games may be canceled as they were in 1916 when
it also was Berlin, strangely
enough, that had been picked as
the Olympic city. The World War
caused this.

Third, the various nations may
refuse to send athletes to the meet.
And as a corollary to the last
item there is a possibility that the
United States would not participate, even if the other nations did.
As far as is known, no definite
word had been received that Hitler
proposes to bar Jews from athletics

Robbins and Wife Regain South African Tennis Titles

JOHANNESBURG, South Afri-
ca, April 17 (AP).—Mr. and Mrs. C.
J. J. Robbins today recovered the
South African men's and women's
singles tennis titles they lost last
year.

Robbins, South African Davis
Cup nominee, defeated the vet-
eran V. G. Kirby in a five-set
final of men's singles, while Mrs.
Robbins, the former Miss R. D.
Tapscott, defeated Mrs. F. H.
Lowe in a three-set final.

Robbins held the title in 1929,
while Mrs. Robbins was champion in 1930.

change overnight. But at any rate

JEWS ASK PROTEST TO GERMANS BY U. S.

Group Representing a Number of Organizations Denounces Reich 'Reign of Terror.'

KING SEEKS INVESTIGATION

Senator Offers Resolution to Set Up Inquiry on Alleged 'Persecution' in Germany.

Special to THE NEW YORK TIMES.

WASHINGTON, July 26.—A protest against the persecution of Jews
in Germany was made to William
Phillips, Acting Secretary of State,
today by a delegation representing
a number of Jewish organizations
who referred also to the "reign of
terror" exercised against Catholics,
Protestants and liberals by the
Nazi government.

The delegation asked that the
United States Government "take all
steps consistent with international
practice to inform the German Government of the outraged sentiments
of our citizens."

"The Olympic protocol provides
there shall be no restriction of competition because of class, color or
creed. The matter will no doubt be
taken up by the American Olympic
Committee."

SHORE IS SELECTED FOR HOCKEY HONORS

Boston Star Voted Most Valu-able Player Prize for Last National League Season.

By The Canadian Press.

MONTREAL, April 17.—Eddie

WOOD IS EXTENDED TO WIN NET MATCH

lace
Kills 4

IMES.
he col-
e house
coverer
ze win-
e years
of four
injuries

ur fire-
at Addis Ababa.

BRUNDAGE FAVORS BERLIN OLYMPICS

U. S. Sports Official Says He Knows of No Reason to Boycott Germany.

HAS FAITH IN NAZI PLEDGE

Holds It Is Too Late to Get New Place for 1936 Games Even if Desired.

Special to THE NEW YORK TIMES.

CHICAGO, July 26.—Avery Brundage, president of the American
Olympic Committee, asserted here
today that he knew of no racial or
religious reasons why the United
States should consider withdrawal
of its athletes from competition at
the Olympic Games in Berlin next
year.

His statement was issued in response to Jeremiah T. Mahoney,
national president of the Amateur
Athletic Union, who was quoted in
New York last night as personally
opposed to participation of all races.

MAHONEY PUSHES PLEA ON OLYMPICS

Objection to Participation in Berlin Games Is Reiterated by Athletic Union Head.

DECRIES BIAS IN SPORTS

Assails Nazi Regime in Talk to Jewish Educators—Aide Presses Participation Plans.

Special to THE NEW YORK TIMES.

WHITE PLAINS, N. Y., July 31.
—Jeremiah T. Mahoney, former Supreme Court Justice and present
head of the Amateur Athletic
Union, renewed tonight his objec-
tion to American participation in
the 1936 Olympic Games at Berlin,
because of German mistreatment of
Jews.

Speaking at a dinner of the Committee of 100 of the Jewish Education Association, Mr. Mahoney,
who is also a member of the American Olympic Committee, declared
that holding the games in Germany
would violate American principles
of sportsmanship. Referring to a
resolution adopted by the A. A. U.
in 1933, to the effect that the
United States would not participate
if it were proved that Germany had
discriminated against Jewish athletes, he said that the A. A. U.
would investigate this question
carefully at its convention in New
York in the Fall.

"I personally will vote against
such participation and I will urge
others to vote against it if any evi-
dence of discrimination is found,"
he said. "The time may come when
the burden will be placed on those
who want the Olympic Games in
their country to prove that they
have not done what they are ac-
cused of doing."

Notes Effect of Bias.

Mr. Mahoney, whose interest in
athletics dates from his youth.

WILL GET TIM

THE NEW Y

sports mine
will not be
ated becau
liefs. We w
where the
there is a C
destinies. '
places whe
reactionarie
give a squa

His prote
directed ag
True friend
could do th
their prote
stroy the p
The dinne
persons, wa
Country Cl

A. A. U. I

Daniel A.
tary-treasur
nounced yes
sociated Pr
an ear to '
to Germany
organization
steadily wit
for full Am
the Olympic

"There h
a change in
sentiment '
plete team
"The A. A
posed to
activities i
a fair deal
can withdra
Olympic G
situation
action.

"There h
however, to
in Germany
cerned. W
our organiz
I believe t
difficulties
now and th
Germany h
holding the
Mr. Ferri
that in an
Olympics is
which is bi
the 1940 ga

"The Oly
called off e
are not held
would be in
precedented

ermany's Campaign Against the Jews

ANHASSET BAY.

SENATORS BEATEN BY RED SOX, 4 TO 2

Henry Johnson Holds Losers to 3 Hits Until 8th in Boston's Initial Victory.

WATWOOD SAVES THE DAY

8 Big League Openers Drew 153,526, Increase of 15,000

Although it required more time than usual to put them on, the eight originally scheduled major league openings have been completed, with an aggregate attendance of 153,526, tabulation by The Associated Press revealed yesterday.

The 1933 total for eight games is 15,000 in excess of the aggregate for the eight openers last

FOX'S HOMER WINS FOR TIGERS IN 10TH

Youngster's Drive With Two on Bases Decides Struggle With White Sox, 8-5.

WHITE DEADLOCKS GAME

"All the News That's

The New York Times.

Copyright, 1935, by The New York Times Company.

PART THREE
THE BOYCOTT DEBATE

VOL. LXXXV....No. 28,443.   Entered as Second-Class Matter, Postoffice, New York, N. Y.   TWO CENTS

A. A. U. BACKS TEAM IN BERLIN OLYMPIC; REJECTS BOYCOTT

MAHONEY FORCES LOSE

Withdraw Motion for Ban as Five-Hour Debate Shows Defeat Sure.

INQUIRY IS VOTED DOWN

Resolution Adopted Calling on Game Committees to See No Injustice Is Done.

BRUNDAGE NEW PRESIDENT

Mahoney Refuses to Run Again —Calls Result Moral Victory and Plans to Fight On.

The general convention of the Amateur Athletic Union of the United States closed at the Hotel Commodore yesterday with a rejection of all attempts to keep American athletes out of the Olympic Games in Germany.

Sister of American Held As Spy Suspect in Spain

By the Associated Press.

MADRID, Dec. 8.—Sarah Abramovitch, 28 years old, sister of Benjamin Aleon of Peoria, Ill., was arrested and held incommunicado today pending hearing on a warrant for her deportation issued by the Department of Public Safety.

The warrant did not specify the charges against her, but jail attendants at the women's prison said she was suspected of espionage.

The girl, a White Russian, has been employed in various parts of Spain for thirty months, translating books and teaching languages. She is understood to have two other brothers who are naturalized Americans living in the United States.

200-INCH 'EYE' BORN WITHOUT A DEFECT

Mirror for World's Largest Telescope Is Removed From Oven at Corning Plant.

CARDINAL IN PULPIT SCORES NEW MOVE FOR BIRTH CONTROL

3,000 in Cathedral Hear Him Insist on the Right of Relief Mothers to Bear Children.

NATION GOING 'DECADENT'

He Declares the Real Problem Is to Provide Economic Sufficiency for the Poor.

The text of Cardinal Hayes's sermon is on Page 5.

Aroused by the recent movement to have birth control information provided for the mothers of families on relief, Cardinal Hayes, Archbishop of New York, occupied the pulpit of St. Patrick's Cathedral at pontifical high mass at 11 o'clock yesterday morning to voice his "measured, deliberate and emphatic condemnation of the effrontery" of its proponents.

It was the first time that Cardinal Hayes had preached the sermon at St. Patrick's since Oct. 25, 1931, and the Cardinal made it abundantly evident that he attached the greatest importance to his sermon. He himself changed the regular assignment to preach at the high mass in order to deliver it.

Cardinal Hayes said that it was with great reluctance that he discussed a topic that he would rather not have taken up in public.

Thick 'Midnight Fog' Dims Lights of the City

A heavy "pea-soup" fog enveloped the city early this morning, accompanied by a sharp change to warmer from the temperature of the last few days. Starting at about 10 o'clock last night, the fog gathered in thick smoke-like billows that were rolling heavily over the city by midnight.

The haze over the brightly lighted Times Square area was so thick that many of the lights were dimmed and wisps of fog could be seen moving slowly in a light wind. The police in the Times Square area and downtown at police headquarters said, it was one of the thickest "midnight fogs" they had ever seen.

Rising temperatures had reached a maximum of 48 by 2 o'clock this morning.

The fog was expected to delay incoming ships. It appeared to have had little effect on street traffic because of the lateness at which it began gathering. Sunday motor traffic, lightened by the rain and cloudy skies of the day, was at a minimum last night.

ONE INCOME IN 1934 TOPPED $5,000,000

In 1929 Peak There Were 38 —32 Last Year Received a Net Over $1,000,000.

'REDISTRIBUTION' IS NOTED

NAVAL TALKS OPEN TODAY WITH PARITY AS THE FIRST ISSUE

France and Italy Will Let the 3 Bigger Powers Take Up Japan's Plea at Outset.

LITTLE ACCORD IN LONDON

British Tend to Allow U. S. to Bear Brunt of the Fight to Preserve Ratio System.

By FREDERICK T. BIRCHALL.
Special Cable to The New York Times.

LONDON, Dec. 8.—The world's chief naval powers, the United States, Great Britain, Japan, France and Italy, will meet in conference here tomorrow in the hope of concluding "a new international treaty for the limitation of naval armaments." Upon the outcome of their deliberations will depend the future expenditures of all countries possessing navies, and this in turn will affect the pockets of hundreds of millions of taxpayers the world over.

Unless the conference reaches an agreement the world is likely to see in the immediate future a renewal of the costly race in armament construction, which has been so expensive in the past and already has proved to be one cause of war.

Yet, despite the most elaborate preliminary negotiations, never before has a conference opened with so small a measure of preliminary agreement among the participation

NEW ETHIOPI FIXED BY HO AS FINAL OF

Italy Would Get Almost Half Under Paris Peace Scheme, M

By AUGUR.
Special Cable to The New York Tim

LONDON, Dec. 8.—The dismemberment cession of almost half her territory to Italy, the British and French Governments this ing effort to make Premier Benito Mussolini Africa.

News reached London tonight from a Sir Samuel Hoare, British Foreign Secretary Laval of France had agreed on terms fav posed by the League Committee of Five ta perts who had been conferring in Paris in re

The two statesmen refused to give Italy and the long-sought corridor between her P but instead they offered her a huge belt o roughly 250 miles broad and between 600 a tending from the British Somaliland frontie Rudolf.

This includes not only the fever-ridden vast tract of healthful highland country watered and suitable for colonization by b would be Long. 26 W. and Lat. 8 S., thus be gion of nine lakes and a considerable area ce under Italian rule.

In the North Italy would receive Ea with Adowa and Makale, but the Ethiopian city of Aksum. Ethiopia would receive the rea, with a corridor of territory leading to indicates that Mussolini would be willing to cess to the sea, but insists on keeping cont hinterland to prevent arms from reaching t

---

Navy Saturday.

to THE NEW YORK TIMES.

OLIS, Md., April 17.—
men of the Massachusetts
of Technology, under
l Haines, arrived today
main for the week as the
the midshipmen, while
for the racing on Satur-
ity, junior varsity, fresh-
150-pound events will be
naval Academy, all
Henley distance.

ns this afternoon were fa-
r practice. All four crews
were on the water and will

tories, which he extended to 16 when he defeated the Athletics in the opening game of the season. The first 15 triumphs were put together last season.

The box score:

BOSTON (A.)

	ab.	r.	h.	po.	a.	e.
Werstler, ss.	4	1	1	2	1	0
R.John'n, rf.	5	1	1	4	0	0
McMan's, 3b.	3	0	1	3	0	0
Alex'der, 1b.	4	1	1	9	0	0
Winsett, rf.	4	1	1	0	0	0
Stumpf, rf.	3	0	0	0	0	0
Watwood, lf.	4	0	2	0	0	0
Hodapp, 2b.	3	0	1	2	4	1
Shea, c.	4	0	0	3	0	0
H.John'n, p.	3	0	1	0	1	0
Kline, p.	0	0	0	0	0	0
Welch, p.	0	0	0	0	0	0
bJolley	1	0	0	0	0	0
Total	**35**	**4**	**9**	**27**	**19**	**1**

WASHINGTON (A.)

	ab.	r.	h.	po.	a.	e.
Kuhel, 1b.	4	1	1	0	0	0
Myer, 2b.	4	3	1	2	3	1
Manush, lf.	4	0	2	3	1	0
Cronin, ss.	2	0	0	3	1	0
Goslin, lf.	3	0	2	2	0	0
Schulte, cf.	4	0	0	2	0	0
Bluege, 3b.	4	0	0	1	2	0
Sewell, c.	4	0	1	6	1	0
Crowder, p.	2	0	0	2	0	0
Burke, p.	0	0	0	0	0	0
Thomas, p.	0	0	0	0	0	0
aRice	1	0	0	0	0	0
cBolton	1	0	0	0	0	0
dHarris	0	0	0	0	0	0
Total						

Decoration Day, Independence Day, Labor Day and Sept. 17. Rain, snow, darkness and a tie, about everything that could happen to a baseball club, have contrived to produce six more.

The first of the postponed Boston games will be played as part of a double-header on April 30.

DODGER GAME PUT OFF.

Bad Weather Adds Double-Header With Braves to Schedule.

Special to THE NEW YORK TIMES.

BOSTON, April 17.—The inclement weather conditions that prevented the Giants from fulfilling any part of their opening schedule

The box score:

CHICAGO (A.)

	ab.	r.	h.	po.	a.	e.
Hayes, 2b.	4	1	0	1	5	0
Haas, cf.	4	1	1	5	0	0
Fonseca, lf.	4	1	1	1	0	0
Simmons, lf.	5	1	2	2	0	0
Appling, ss.	4	0	0	2	3	1
Kress, rf.	4	1	1	1	0	0
Dykes, 3b.	4	1	0	1	1	0
Cruise, c.	3	0	1	5	0	0
Gaston, p.	3	0	0	0	0	0
Frasier, p.	0	0	0	0	0	0
Total	**35**	**5**	**7**	**29**	**15**	**1**

DETROIT (A.)

	ab.	r.	h.	po.	a.	e.
Davis, 1b.	5	0	2	10	0	0
Owen, 3b.	5	2	3	2	3	0
Gehr'ger, 2b.	4	0	1	3	5	0
Stone, rf.	4	2	0	3	0	0
White, lf.	5	1	2	1	0	0
Fox, cf.	5	2	2	5	0	0
Rogell, ss.	4	0	1	3	5	0
Hayworth, c.	4	0	1	4	1	0
Sorrell, p.	2	0	0	0	0	0
Herring, p.	0	0	0	1	1	0
Wyatt, p.	0	0	0	0	0	0
Marberry, p.	1	0	0	0	1	0
aWebb	0	0	0	0	0	0
bWalker	1	1	0	0	0	0
Total	**39**	**8**	**12**	**30**	**14**	**0**

*Two out when winning runs scored.
aBatted for Herring in third.
bBatted for Wyatt in eighth.

Chicago .... 5 0 0   0 0 0   0 0 0—5
Detroit .... 0 0 0   1 0 0   0 4 0   3—8

SHOULD THE GAMES GO ON?

After Hitler became dictator of Germany, many Americans and citizens of other western democracies, outraged by the actions of the Nazis, questioned whether their countries should still send teams to Berlin. Leaders in the Olympics movement were dismayed when they learned that some Nazis were calling for the removal of both Dr. Theodor Lewald and German sports leader Carl Diem from the German committee organizing the Berlin Games. Like Lewald, Diem had Jewish ties—his wife had one Jewish grandparent. International Olympic Committee president Baillet-Latour warned Hitler that the Olympics would not take place in Berlin unless Lewald and Diem remained on the organizing committee. Hitler bowed to pressure, showing the importance he placed on hosting the Games. Nonetheless, both men were stripped of their positions in the German sports world: Lewald lost his position as president of the German Olympic Committee to the Nazi Tschammer

Avery Brundage (1887–1975) grew up fatherless and poor in Chicago. He distinguished himself as an athlete and student, graduating from the University of Illinois. He participated in the pentathlon and decathlon in the 1912 Stockholm Games. A civil engineer, he made a fortune in the Chicago construction industry. In 1928 Brundage was elected president of the Amateur Athletic Union, a position he held, except for the year 1933, until 1935, and president of its Olympic arm, the American Olympic Association (later known as the American Olympic Committee). *University of Illinois Archives, Champaign-Urbana, Ill.*

und Osten, and Diem was dismissed from his job as administrator in a sports college he had helped found.

Reports of Nazi discrimination against Jewish athletes then became the central issue in a debate that developed over participation in the Berlin Olympics. The question was most hotly argued in the United States, which historically sent one of the largest teams to the Games. After every Summer Olympics between 1920 and 1932—at Antwerp, Paris, Amsterdam, and Los Angeles— American athletes brought home the most medals. Passing up the chance to do the same at Berlin would be a sacrifice for athletes, their coaches, and American Olympics organizers.

The president of the American Olympic Committee (AOC), Avery Brundage, at first questioned whether the 1936 Olympics should be held in Berlin. Like many others in the international Olympics movement, for a while he considered the idea of moving the Games from Germany. In an interview in mid-April 1933, Brundage said, "My personal, but unofficial opinion is that the Games will not be held in any country where there will be inter-

The establishment of "Olympic training courses" for Jewish athletes in 1934 was a sham, part of the Nazi effort to deflect international criticism about discrimination against Jewish athletes. No one from these courses, including Gretel Bergmann (*foreground*) would participate in the Olympics. Bergmann had returned to Germany from England after German officials hinted that her family would be in trouble if she did not do as they wished. *Dr. George Eisen.*

ference with the fundamental Olympic theory of equality of all races. The Olympic protocol provides there shall be no restriction of competition because of class, color, or creed." Brundage supported the position taken by the Amateur Athletic Union (AAU) in November 1933 to decline the invitation to Berlin unless German Jewish athletes were allowed to train and compete for the Olympics. The AAU's stand was important, because this organization, along with the AOC, determined which American athletes qualified for the Olympic team.

In the middle of 1934, the Nazi government attempted to show that German Jewish athletes were being treated fairly. Reich Sports Office leader Tschammer un Osten announced that twenty-one Jews, including high jumper Gretel Bergmann, had been invited to train at special Olympic courses. That September, Brundage went to Germany to see for himself whether Jewish athletes were enjoying equal opportunity to compete for the German Olympic team. After only a brief tour of German sports facilities—carefully controlled by German Karl Ritter von Halt of

Karl Ritter von Halt (1891–1964) competed in the 1912 Olympics. He received his title of nobility in 1917 for bravery during World War I. He was several times German decathlon champion and from 1924 to 1939 a coach of track and field. An International Olympic Committee member from 1929, he headed the organizing committee for the 1936 Winter Games. Halt was a Nazi Party member and during World War II a major general of the SA storm troopers. In spite of his close ties to the Nazi regime, Halt regained a leadership role in the IOC after the war with the support of his old friend, then IOC president, Avery Brundage.

Avery Brundage (*left*) is shown at a pre-Olympics reception with Karl Ritter von Halt, of the International Olympic Committee. Ritter von Halt escorted Brundage during his 1934 investigation into the situation of Jewish athletes. Berlin, Germany, July 1936. *Ullstein Bilderdienst, Berlin, Germany.*

the IOC and other Nazi officials who acted as guides — Brundage stated publicly that Jewish athletes were being treated fairly and that the Games should go on as planned. On September 26, 1934, the AOC officially accepted the German Olympic Committee's invitation to the 1936 Olympics.

SUPPORT FOR A BOYCOTT

The president of the Amateur Athletic Union, Jeremiah Mahoney, opposed U.S. participation in the 1936 Olympics. In 1935, spurred by attacks on Jews in Berlin that July and by the announcement of anti-Jewish laws in Nuremberg that September, he began publicly supporting a boycott of the Games. Mahoney said that Nazi ideology—based on racial inequality—was the direct opposite of the Olympic code, which was based on the equality of all races and of all faiths in the area of sports. He warned, "I believe that for America to participate in the Olympics in Germany means giving American moral and financial support to the Nazi regime, which is opposed to all that Americans hold dearest." Mahoney's feelings were shared by liberal Catholic leaders Al Smith, governor of New York, and James Curley, governor of Massachusetts, and by a number of other Catholics as well as Protestants who viewed the Nazis as anti-Christian. Many Jewish organizations, trade union leaders, and other anti-Nazis also

Former New York State Supreme Court Justice Jeremiah Mahoney (*right*), president of the Amateur Athletic Union, opposed American participation in the Olympics. Avery Brundage (*left*), president of the American Olympic Committee, supported participation. The disagreement destroyed their friendship. *UPI/Corbis-Bettmann, New York, N.Y.*

American trade unionists in New York City at a November 1935 rally in support of the Olympics boycott. *UPI/Corbis-Bettmann, New York, N.Y.*

TRADE UNIONISTS!

JOIN ANTI-NAZI PARADE NOV. 21st

SUPPORT THE AMERICAN FEDERATION OF LABOR RESOLUTION TO BOYCOTT THE 1936 OLYMPICS IN NAZI GERMANY!

MARCH AGAINST THE NAZIS

Thursday, Nov. 21st, at 4 p.m.

Gather at 33rd to 40th Sts. W. of 8th Ave., N.Y.

March to Madison Sq. Park where a Gigantic MASS MEETING will begin at 7 P.M.

NAZISM IS PUBLIC ENEMY No. 1 OF THE LABOR MOVEMENT!

10,000 German trade unionists, leaders and rank and filers are in exile, it was reported at the last convention of the American Federation of Labor.

Thousands more were thrown into concentration camps!

Sixty-one year old Fritz Husemann, President of the German Miners Union, was beaten to death in a concentration camp.

"Tortured to death" and "beaten to death" was the fate of scores for the crime of being trade union members.

Calling for a boycott of the Olympics, the Convention of the American Federation of Labor, held in Atlantic City, declared:

"The powerful German trade union movement was stamped out in blood and fire in order to clear the way for an attack upon the living standards of the German working class."

"We stand with bowed heads before the graves of the many true and tried leaders of labor who were killed in cold blood for their allegiance to labor by Nazi gangsters and we extend a hand of friendship to those in exile or in prison and concentration camps."

"We call upon all American sports organizations not to participate in the Olympic games. Such participation would only be used to confer prestige on the Nazi regime."

WILLIAM GREEN, President of the American Federaion of Labor, says: "Born in blood, the Nazi regime thrives on force and moves onward in hopes of war and conquest. For the sake of the human race and for its own sake, labor must combat it and must strengthen the hands of all its true opponents."

At its convention on December 5th, the Amateur Athletic Union will vote on whether or not the United States shall send its teams to Nazi Germany.

Hitler will utilize the presence of the Olympics as a tribunal from which to call the youth of the world — a call which can only further the Nazi war plans.

● Do your bit to strike a blow at Nazi barbarism!

● Liberate the race, religious, labor and other anti-Nazi prisoners held in Nazi concentration camps!

● Free the leaders of the German Labor, peace and church movement: Brandes, Huebke, Carl Von Ossietzky, Ernst Thaelmann and Mierendorf.

● Answer General Sherill! Raise your voice for U. S. withdrawal from the Olympic games!

ANTI-NAZI FEDERATION, 168 W. 23rd St., N.Y.C. Telephone: CHelsea 2-3759

supported a boycott of the Olympics as part of their wider support of an economic boycott of all German products.

Mahoney's Committee on Fair Play in Sports published a pamphlet that made the case for a boycott and organized public meetings and letter-writing campaigns in support of the cause. A number of former Olympians joined the committee, including speed skater Jack Shea, a gold medalist at the 1932 Winter Games at

THE MODERN MERCURY.　　　—By Jerry Doyle

This cartoon by Jerry Doyle appeared in a pamphlet entitled "Preserve the Olympic Ideal: A Statement of the Case Against American Participation in the Olympic Games at Berlin," published by Mahoney's Committee on Fair Play in Sports. The cartoon suggests that Nazism and the 1936 Olympics were a betrayal of the Olympic ideals of sportsmanship and international goodwill. *The 1932 & 1980 Lake Placid Winter Olympic Museum, Lake Placid, New York.*

Lake Placid, and Jim Bausch, decathlon winner at Los Angeles in 1932. Forty-one college presidents from more than twenty states also publicly declared their support for a boycott. Ernest Lee Jahncke, an American member of the International Olympic Committee, spoke out publicly against going to Berlin. The son of German Protestant immigrants to the United States and a former assistant secretary of the navy, Jahncke was horrified at developments in Nazi Germany and what he considered an obvious use of the Games by the Nazis for propaganda. His outspoken stance infuriated IOC leaders, who would expel him from the body in July 1936.

In the face of growing opposition to participation, AOC president Avery Brundage fought hard to send a U.S. team to the 1936 Olympics, stating, "The Olympic Games belong to the athletes and not to the politicians." He wrote in a pamphlet "Fair Play for American Athletes," published by the AOC, that American athletes should not become involved in a "Jew-Nazi" fight. On December 8, 1935, Brundage was able to claim final victory when a proposal to boycott the Olympics was defeated at a meeting of the Amateur Athletic Union in New York. The vote was extremely close, but a determined Brundage maneuvered the process to achieve success. He may also have been aided by the announcement in late 1935 that fencer Helene Mayer had accepted the German Olympic

Ernest Lee Jahncke (1877–1960) was one of three U.S. members of the International Olympic Committee. His father had emigrated from Germany to New Orleans in 1869 and made a fortune in shipbuilding. Ernest Jahncke became one of America's top yachtsmen and an assistant secretary of the navy under President Herbert Hoover. He was invited to join the American Olympic Committee in 1926 and a year later was elected to the International Olympic Committee. In a letter to IOC president Baillet-Latour published in the *New York Times* on November 27, 1935, Jahncke wrote that he believed the Nazi government and German sports authorities had not given Jewish athletes a fair opportunity to compete for the German team and were exploiting the games for the political and financial profit of the Nazi regime. "Neither Americans, nor the representatives of other countries," he wrote, "can take part in the games in Nazi Germany without at least acquiescing in the contempt of the Nazis for fair play and their sordid exploitation of the games." *The Historic New Orleans Collection, New Orleans, La.*

Committee's invitation to compete on the German Olympic team. In 1936 IOC leaders would reward Brundage for his vital support by giving him Jahncke's place on the committee.

At no time did U.S. President Franklin D. Roosevelt become involved in the boycott debate. Both the American ambassador to Germany, William E. Dodd, and George Messersmith, head of the U.S. Legation in Vienna, opposed the American Olympic Committee's decision to go to Berlin. They wrote long, detailed reports to the U.S. State Department in Washington in which they explained that the Nazi government had taken over the Olympics for its own purposes, which were opposed to the Olympic ideal, and that "Olympic training courses" for Jewish athletes were a clear attempt to deceive the world. Messersmith wrote, "I am of the opinion that the American Olympic Committee, in taking the stand which it has, has failed in its duty towards the young people of our country." But his and Dodd's reports failed to get the State Department or the president to speak out against the Berlin Olympics. Roosevelt continued a forty-year tradition in which the American Olympic Committee operated independently of outside influence. Ignoring requests from the committee, Roosevelt did not give the Olympic team a good-bye telephone call or agree to a radio hookup when the athletes sailed for Berlin. Nor did he invite the team to the White House after its return.

AFRICAN AMERICAN VOICES

After the International Olympic Committee received pledges from German leaders that black athletes would be treated well at Berlin, most African American newspapers supported participation in the 1936 Olympics. Writers for such papers as the *Philadelphia Tribune* and the *Chicago Defender* argued that athletic victories by blacks would disprove Nazi racial views of "Aryan" supremacy and promote a new sense of black pride at home. In 1936 a large number of black athletes were Olympic contenders, and in the end, nineteen African Americans — seventeen men and two women — went to Berlin. This was three times the number who had competed in the 1932 Lost Angeles Games.

For these black athletes, the Olympics provided a special opportunity. In the 1930s, blacks suffered discrimination in most areas of American life. "Jim Crow" laws, designed by whites to keep blacks powerless and segregated, barred African Americans

The *Chicago Defender*, December 14, 1935, reported that African American track stars Eulace Peacock, Jesse Owens (*left*), and Ralph Metcalfe (*right*) favored participating in the Olympics because they felt that their victories would serve to repudiate Nazi racial theories. *AP/Wide World Photos, New York, N.Y.*

from many jobs and from entering public places such as restaurants and hotels. In the area of sports, opportunities for blacks were also limited, at both the college and professional levels. Black journalists criticized supporters of the Olympic boycott for talking so much about discrimination against athletes in foreign lands but not addressing the problem of discrimination against

This cartoon by "Holloway" from the African American newspaper the *Pittsburgh Courier* provided a rousing send-off for black Olympians who sailed with the rest of their team for Germany on the cruise ship SS *Manhattan*, July 18, 1939. *By permission of GRM Associates, Inc., New York, N.Y.*

athletes at home. Pointing out that all the black Olympians came from northern universities that served mostly white students, they said that this showed the inferiority of training equipment and facilities at traditionally black colleges, where most African American students were educated in the 1930s.

Professional boxing was among the few integrated sports in

Jesse Owens (1913–1980) was born in Alabama, the second youngest of eleven children of poor sharecroppers. When Owens was nine, the family moved to Cleveland, Ohio. His greatest athletic achievement before the Olympics came at a Big Ten meet in Ann Arbor, Michigan, on May 25, 1935. Before spellbound spectators, Owens broke five world records and equaled another. In November 1935, several weeks after the Nazis proclaimed the anti-Jewish "Nuremberg Laws," Owens publicly spoke of withdrawing from the Games. But his coach, Larry Snyder, advised him not to take any position or risk becoming a "forgotten man." In vain *Call and Post,* a black weekly in Cleveland, urged Owens to stay away from Games being staged by "the world's outstanding criminal gang, the Nazis."

Water fountain for "colored" persons only. Halifax, North Carolina, April 1938. *Library of Congress, Washington, D.C.*

The "Rex Theatre for Colored People" was a segregated cinema in Leland, Mississippi, June 1937. *Library of Congress, Washington, D.C.*

Ralph Metcalfe (1910–1978) was born in Atlanta, Georgia, moved with his family to Chicago, and attended Marquette University in Milwaukee, Wisconsin. One of the top track stars of the 1930s, Metcalfe won the silver medal in the 100-meter and took third in the 200-meter race at the 1932 Olympics. Aboard ship on the way to Berlin in 1936, the highly respected Metcalfe spoke before a meeting of the black track and field athletes, urging them to avoid political discussions in Europe. He said their goal was simply to win, for themselves, for their schools, and for their country. After the Olympics, Metcalfe coached track at Xavier, a historically black college in New Orleans. From 1970 to 1978 Metcalfe represented the First District of Illinois in the U.S. House of Representatives.

Champions Negro National League 1935

the United States, and prizefighter Joe Louis was a hero to African Americans. Less than two months before the Summer Olympics, Louis was knocked out in a fight against the German Max Schmeling. Hitler's Minister of Propaganda, Joseph Goebbels, trumpeted Schmeling's victory as a triumph for Germany. One Nazi newspaper commented, "Schmeling's victory was not only sport. It was a question of prestige for our race." Schmeling, who was never a Nazi, was present at many festivities during the Berlin Olympics. In a 1938 rematch, Louis would defeat Schmeling in one round.

The Pittsburgh Crawfords were 1935 champions of the Negro leagues. Blacks were barred from professional baseball until 1947, professional football until 1946, professional basketball until 1950, and professional golf until 1961. *AP/Wide World Photos, New York, N.Y., provided by the National Baseball Hall of Fame and Museum, Inc., Cooperstown, N.Y.*

AMERICAN JEWISH VOICES

Beginning in 1933, two American Jewish groups — the American Jewish Congress and the Jewish Labor Committee — joined by the Anti-Nazi League, made up of Jews and non-Jews, staged mass rallies to protest Nazi persecution of Jews, political opponents, and others. These groups supported the boycott of the 1936 Games as part of a larger boycott of German goods. Rabbi Stephen Wise, president of the American Jewish Congress, fought an uphill battle in the 1930s to inform the American government and people about the evils of Nazism. Rabbi Wise publicly supported an Olympics boycott and urged Jewish athletes not to participate. He was joined by rabbis and other Jewish leaders across the United States who urged athletes and others to support a boycott.

After being informed about discrimination against Jews and Jewish athletes in Germany, a number of American Jewish athletes withdrew from Olympic trials. They included Herman Neu-

gass, a sprinter at Tulane University in New Orleans, Milton Green, captain of the Harvard University track team, and his college roommate Norman Cahners, also a track star, and the Long Island University basketball team, composed of Jews and non-Jews who voted to boycott the Olympic basketball trials.

Some Jewish groups, such as the American Jewish Committee and B'nai B'rith, did not publicly support a boycott of the Berlin

Nazi supporters give the Hitler salute at a Madison Square Garden rally opposing the boycott of German goods that had been organized by anti-Nazi groups in the United States, May 18, 1934. *UPI/Corbis-Bettmann, New York, N.Y.*

Milton Green (1913–) grew up in Brookline, Massachusetts, and attended Temple Israel in Boston. In 1936 he and his Harvard College roommate Norman Cahners, who was also Jewish, together won six events at the Harvard-Yale track meet. Green won the high hurdles, the low hurdles, and the running broad jump (now called the long jump). They qualified for the final Olympic trials to be held at Randall's Island a few weeks before the Games. But after reading about the athletes in a Boston newspaper, Rabbi Levy from Temple Israel met with them to inform them about the ongoing mistreatment of Jews and others in Germany. Green later recalled that since he had not had a detailed understanding of the problems in Germany, the meeting was a "shocker" to him and Cahners. They then told their track coach they were not going to Randall's Island. Their coach tried but failed to change their minds. *Milton Green.*

Herman Neugass (1915–1991) grew up in New Orleans, Louisiana, and entered Tulane University in 1931. He quickly became the school's and one of the country's top sprinters. He declined to try out for the Olympics, however, after hearing about the September 1935 "Nuremberg Laws." That December, he wrote the *New Orleans Times-Picayune* that he had been informed on what he believed to be "unimpeachable authority" that German pledges of nondiscrimination among the athletes of that country had "not been kept." He

said, "I feel it to be my duty to express my unequivocal opinion that this country should not participate in the Olympic contests, if they are held in Germany." The Olympic track and field coach Lawson Robertson wrote to the Jewish sprinter, asking him to reconsider: "I want to tell you that we take seven sprinters, that is three for the 100 meters and four for the short relay. I am quite certain that there are not seven people who can beat you." But Neugass held firm. *Richard Neugass.*

American Jewish sprinter Herman Neugass chose to boycott the 1936 Olympic trials because of Nazi discrimination against Jewish athletes. *Richard Neugass.*

During the 1930s, employers discriminated against Jews in hiring, as shown in this "help wanted" advertisement from the *New York Herald Tribune*, August 11, 1938, seeking only "Christian" applicants for various female clerical jobs.

During the 1930s, American Jews faced discrimination in many areas of everyday life. Hotels, like this one in New York State's Adirondacks, publicly stated "Applications from Hebrews not desired," c. 1930. *The Adirondack Museum, Blue Mountain Lake, N.Y.*

Olympics. They feared that such a stand might fuel antisemitism in both Germany and the United States. During the 1930s, prejudice toward Jews was widespread in American culture and everyday social life. Employers discriminated against Jews in hiring, universities limited the number of Jewish students through informal admission quotas, and certain neighborhoods and social clubs barred Jews. As an example of more extreme antisemitism, the "radio priest" Father Charles Coughlin attacked Jews on his national program, which reached millions of listeners.

Actively fueling extreme antisemitism, the "radio priest" Father Charles Coughlin maligned Jews on his national program that reached millions of listeners. *AP/Wide World Photos, New York, N.Y.*

WORLD VOICES

Limited support for a boycott of the 1936 Olympics developed in Canada, Great Britain, France, Sweden, Czechoslovakia, and the Netherlands. German Socialists and Communists in exile voiced their opposition to the Games through publications such as *Arbeiter Illustrierte Zeitung* (The Worker Illustrated Newspaper), printed in Czechoslovakia.

A number of counter-Olympics were also planned in Europe. One of the largest was "The People's Olympiad" in Barcelona, Spain. Scheduled to open in July 1936, it was canceled after the outbreak of the Spanish Civil War, just as thousands of athletes began to arrive. This Olympiad, like Games held in Prague, Czechoslovakia, carried on a tradition of sports festivals staged by working-class groups linked to left-wing political parties.

Individual Jewish athletes from around the world also chose to boycott the Berlin Olympics. Former gymnast Gustav Felix Flatow,

de olympiade onder dictatuur

D-O-O-D

tentoonstelling:
sport, kunst, wetenschap, documenten

amsterdam
augustus
1936
gebouw
de geelvinck
singel 530

de olympiade onder dictatuur

This poster advertises a counter-Olympics art festival, "The Olympics Under Dictatorship," held in Amsterdam in August 1936; D-O-O-D spells "death" in Dutch. Following pressure put on Dutch officials by the Nazi government, the exhibition closed in October 1936. *Bibliothek der Friedrich-Ebert-Stiftung, Bonn, Germany; University of Illinois Archives, Champaign-Urbana, Ill.; International Institute for Social History, Amsterdam, The Netherlands.*

a medalist for Germany's first Olympic team in 1896, rejected an official invitation to attend the 1936 Games as an honored guest. Three swimmers named to the Austrian Olympic team, Judith Deutsch, Ruth Langer, and Lucie Goldner, did not join their team in Berlin. Philippe de Rothschild, a Jewish bobsledder from France, boycotted the 1936 Winter Games held in Garmisch-Partenkirchen, Germany. Yisrael "Sammy" Luftspring, the top-ranked lightweight

Judith Deutsch was one of three Jewish swimmers named to the Austrian team who chose to boycott the Olympics. 1930–36. *John Bunzl,* Hoppauf Hakoah *(Vienna, 1987).*

Ruth Langer (1922–1999) was only fifteen years old when she became Austrian champion in 1936 in the 100- and 400-meter freestyle races. A member of the Austrian Jewish sports association Hakoah (meaning "strength"), Langer heeded the advice of the World Federation of Jewish Sports Clubs not to participate in the Olympics hosted by Nazi Germany. Antisemitism was strong in Austria at the time, and the Federation of Austrian Swimming Clubs punished Langer and her Jewish teammates Judith Deutsch and Lucie Goldner for their action by banning them from all competitions for life and stripping them of their official records "due to severe damage of Austrian sports" and "gross disregard for the Olympic spirit." After the German invasion of Austria in 1938, Langer fled to Italy, and in 1939, to England, where she won the last long-distance swimming championship in the Thames River. Only in 1995 did the Federation of Austrian Swimming Clubs apologize to Langer and restore her name to the record books. *Austrian Institute for Contemporary History.*

Philippe de Rothschild, the French Jewish bobsledder who boycotted the 1936 Winter Games held in Garmisch-Partenkirchen. Here he is shown in St. Moritz, Switzerland, at the 1928 Winter Games. *Joan Littlewood,* Baron Philippe *(New York, 1984).*

boxer in Canada, decided not to compete in the Olympic trials, and Norman "Babe" Yack, another promising Jewish Canadian boxer, also opposed the Games. In a letter to the *Toronto Globe* dated July 6, 1936, Luftspring and Yack wrote, "We would have been very [loath] to hurt the feelings of our fellow Jews, by going to a land that would exterminate them if it could."

But once the Amateur Athletic Union of the United States voted in December 1935 for participation at Berlin, other countries fell in line. Forty-nine teams from around the world competed in the 1936 Olympics, more than in any previous Games (see Appendix 2). The American team had 312 members, second in size only to Germany's, with 348 athletes. The Soviet Union did not participate in the Berlin Games or any Olympiad until the 1952 Helsinki Games.

Members of the U.S. Olympic team prepare to hoist the Olympic flag on their ship, the SS *Manhattan*. American Olympic president Avery Brundage (*center, wearing glasses and straw hat*) led the delegation that sailed for Europe July 15, 1936. *UPI/Corbis-Bettmann, New York, N.Y., provided by University of Illinois Archives, Champaign-Urbana, Ill.*

Yisrael "Sammy" Luftspring (1916–) was one of the best boxers in his weight class in Canada. An amateur, he won 105 of 110 matches before retiring because of a bad eye injury. Proud of being Jewish, he competed with an embroidered Star of David on his shorts. His parents opposed his trying out for the 1936 Olympics because they feared for his life if he went to Berlin. After Luftspring decided to obey his parents and boycott the Olympic trials in Montreal, he convinced Norman "Babe" Yack, another Jewish boxer, to do the same. Together they wrote the *Toronto Globe*, expressing their "keen disappointment" at having to "turn down the opportunity of trying for the great honour and privilege of making a place on the Canadian team." But they believed that no athlete would think of "engaging in a sporting contest with a bully who would ill-treat even a dumb animal." The German government, in their view, was treating their "brothers and sisters worse than dogs." *Dr. George Eisen.*

Spectators in the Olympic stadium give the Nazi salute, August 1, 1936.
National Archives and Records Administration, College Park, Md.

PART FOUR

THE NAZI OLYMPICS

A PERFECT ARENA FOR THE NAZI PROPAGANDA MACHINE

When the American Olympic team arrived in Berlin on July 24, 1936—a week before opening ceremonies—they received a warm welcome. Thousands of Berliners came out to greet them. German organizers had carefully planned every event leading up to the Olympics, the athletic competition itself, and surrounding festivities. Some Germans had worked years to prepare the Berlin Olympics and received with great relief the news that the United States in the end had decided to bring a team to Berlin.

Nazi leaders also escaped the blow to German prestige that would have resulted if a boycott had succeeded. For three years, they, too, had been preparing for the Games. This sports festival was the perfect arena for the Nazis and their propaganda machine. Even before Hitler took power in 1933, the Nazis had effectively used torch-lit parades and large public rallies to attract Germans, especially young people, who joined the party and its organizations in great numbers.

Storm troopers marching during a torch-lit parade at the Brandenburg Gate in Berlin on the occasion of Hitler's appointment as chancellor, January 30, 1933. *Bundesarchiv Koblenz, Germany.*

When applied to the 1936 Olympics, Nazi "propaganda" also refers to the effort to deceive foreign athletes, journalists, and spectators by showing only the positive side of life in Hitler's "new Germany." Visitors saw colorful advertising posters and beautifully decorated, clean streets. They read only glowing reports about athletes from all nations published in special Olympic newspapers. During the day they attended thrilling athletic events that took place in new, well-designed facilities and in the evening were entertained at lavish parties hosted by welcoming Nazi leaders. What visitors did not see behind this facade of hospitality was the censorship of German newspapers and other media to make sure that nothing was said to offend the guests. They did not see the brutal dictatorship in action, imprisoning its enemies in concentration camps and re-arming for war to acquire new territory for the "Aryan master race."

THE WINTER GAMES: REHEARSAL FOR BERLIN

From February 6 to February 16, 1936, Germany also hosted the Winter Olympics, at Garmisch-Partenkirchen in the Bavarian Alps. This was just the fourth Winter Olympics held. More than one thousand athletes from twenty-nine nations competed. A less prestigious event than the Summer Games, the Winter Olympics provided international Olympic leaders, German Olympic organizers, and Hitler's regime a rehearsal for August, when many more foreign eyes would be turned on Germany and the Olympics.

German officials took several steps to present Germany in a positive light to visitors at Garmisch-Partenkirchen. First, much to the shock of some Nazis, the Reich Sports Office invited Rudi Ball, who was part Jewish, to compete on the nation's ice hockey team. Ball was the only "non-Aryan" on Germany's team in the Winter Olympics, but his participation served its purpose of appearing to meet Olympic ideals of fair play. The concerns of the

This sign, which reads "Admission of Jews is Forbidden!," hung at a ski club in Garmisch-Partenkirchen. It was removed after International Olympic Committee president Henri de Baillet-Latour complained to Hitler. 1936. *AP/Wide World Photos, New York, N.Y.*

International Olympic Committee were also heeded when at President Baillet-Latour's request Hitler ordered anti-Jewish signs in Garmisch-Partenkirchen removed from public view during the Games. Throughout the ten-day winter festival, Hitler served as a gracious host and gave no political speeches. Still, Nazi propaganda efforts to deceive the world were not totally successful. Western journalists observed and reported army troops carrying out exercises at Garmisch. As a result, the Nazi regime would try to downplay the military presence at the Summer Olympics.

The lasting hero of the Winter Olympics was the Norwegian figure skater Sonja Henie, the winner of ten straight world cham-

pionships between 1927 and 1937 and the gold-medal winner in women's singles at Garmisch-Partenkirchen. The blonde Henie, "the Queen of Ice," was frequently seen with Hitler, as they both enjoyed the favorable publicity. After the Olympics, Henie became a multimillionaire Hollywood movie star and producer of ice skating shows.

Sonja Henie and Adolf Hitler at the Ice Palace in Munich, not far from Garmisch-Partenkirchen, where they were first photographed together in 1934. *World Figure Skating Museum, Colorado Springs, Colo.*

THE REMILITARIZATION OF THE RHINELAND

Only twelve days after the Winter Olympics — on March 7, 1936 — German troops crossed the Rhine River and entered the demilitarized zone in the Rhineland. After World War I, by terms of the Treaty of Versailles, the victorious western nations had forced German soldiers to withdraw from this thirty-mile-wide area of southwestern Germany. The aim was to create a buffer zone between Germany and western Europe.

By ordering troops into the Rhineland, Hitler ignored both the Treaty of Versailles and the Locarno Pact of 1925, which again recognized a demilitarized Rhineland. Hitler took a great chance but correctly gambled that France would not risk another war by moving against Germany. He later called the two days after the move into the Rhineland "the most nerve-racking in my life. If the French had marched into the Rhineland, we would have had to withdraw with our tails between our legs, for the military

German citizens welcome German soldiers as they march into the formerly demilitarized Rhineland, March 1936. *UPI/Corbis-Bettmann, New York, N.Y.*

Jerry Doyle's cartoon "The Watch on the Rhine" shows French tank units standing still and watching as German soldiers trample on the Treaty of Versailles and Locarno Pact that prohibited the presence of German troops in the Rhineland. *The* Philadelphia Record, *March 10, 1936.*

resources at our disposal would have been wholly inadequate for even a moderate resistance."

The Nazi regime's aggressive move into the Rhineland revealed Hitler's intention to expand Germany's territory through military conquest. But his actions did not affect plans for Germany to host the Summer Olympics only five months away.

NAZI PROPAGANDA AND THE SUMMER OLYMPICS

A few weeks before the Berlin Olympics opened, a high official in Germany's Ministry of Propaganda told members of the German National Tourist Association, "There has never before been developed a propaganda campaign equal to that of the Olympic Games. . . . The foreigner who comes to us shall see the German people united under its leader, Hitler. Tourism is an important weapon in the struggle for the re-establishment of Germany's world rank."

Recognizing the importance of attracting foreign visitors to Berlin, Germany skillfully promoted the Olympics with colorful posters and magazine articles. In these advertisements, artists often drew a link between Nazi Germany and ancient Greece. These images spoke not only to the Greek origins of the Olympics but also to the Nazi racial myth that the superior German civilization was the rightful heir to an "Aryan" culture of classical antiquity.

The special Olympics issue of the German newsweekly *Die Woche* (The Week), July–August 1936. *John Loaring.*

Germany's propaganda machine also made certain that once foreigners arrived in Berlin, they would not read or hear any news that would cast Germany in a bad light. The Reich Press Chamber under Minister of Propaganda Joseph Goebbels strictly censored the German press, radio, and film industries. In the weeks prior to and during the Summer Olympics, the Chamber issued many orders to German journalists about the language to be used when reporting on the Games. On July 16, 1936, for

NUMBER 14

OLYMPIC GAMES 1936

The Nazis reduced their vision of classical antiquity to ideal "Aryan" racial types: heroic, blue-eyed blonds with finely chiseled features. The magazine *Olympic Games 1936* was published by the Publicity Commission for the XIth Olympic Games, Berlin 1936, for an English-speaking audience. *Amateur Athletic Foundation of Los Angeles, Calif.*

example, reporters were told, "Press coverage should not mention that there are two non-Aryans among the women [on the German team]: Helene Mayer [fencing] and Gretel Bergmann [high jump and all-around track and field competition]."

BERLIN: THE FACADE OF HOSPITALITY

In August 1936, Olympic flags and swastikas hung from the monuments and houses of a festive, crowded Berlin. Most tourists were unaware of the Nazi campaign against Jews, which had been briefly suspended. The regime had removed anti-Jewish signs until the Games were over, and *Der Stürmer* (The Stormer), a rabidly anti-Jewish newspaper, was removed from newsstands. (The paper was still published, though, using racist caricatures of both Jews and blacks in its special Olympics issue.)

Neither did tourists know about a police "cleanup" that swept eight hundred Gypsies off the streets on July 16, 1936, and imprisoned them in a camp in a Berlin suburb or about a huge concentration camp, Sachsenhausen, that was under construction outside Berlin. The population of Sachsenhausen when it opened that fall consisted of political opponents of the Nazi regime, including liberals, Socialists, and Communists, as well as several hundred Jehovah's Witnesses. Nor were visitors aware

that in preparation for the arrival of Olympic spectators, Nazi officials had ordered that foreign homosexuals should not be arrested for a broad range of behaviors between men that were ordinarily considered a crime.

Heinrich Dickerman, a Jehovah's Witness, was among the earliest prisoners of Sachsenhausen concentration camp. The Nazi regime persecuted the Witnesses because their beliefs prohibited them from swearing allegiance to any worldly government. The Witnesses would not raise their arms in the "Heil, Hitler!" salute or join the army. Heinrich's brother, August, was also a prisoner of Sachsenhausen, and in 1939, Heinrich and other Witnesses were forced to watch his execution, one of the first at the camp. August Dickerman was shot for refusing to perform military service. *Robert Buckley.*

ABOVE: Under construction during the Summer Olympics, Sachsenhausen accepted its first prisoners in the fall of 1936. The initial camp population consisted primarily of political opponents of the Nazi regime as well as several hundred Jehovah's Witnesses. *Fotothek der Gedenkstätte und Museum Sachsenhausen, Oranienburg, Germany.*

In this cartoon, artist David Low comments on the Nazi efforts to deceive the world by abstaining from persecuting the Jews during the Olympics. *David Low, Evening Standard, Centre for the Study of Cartoons and Caricature, University of Kent at Canterbury, United Kingdom.*

THE OPENING OF THE GAMES

On Saturday, August 1, 1936, the opening ceremonies of the Summer Olympics took place at four o'clock in the afternoon in a stadium filled with 110,000 people. Musical fanfares directed by the composer Richard Strauss announced Hitler's arrival to the largely German crowd. Hundreds of athletes in opening-day uniforms marched into the stadium, team by team in alphabetical order. Inaugurating a new Olympic ritual, German middle-distance runner Fritz Schilgen arrived bearing a lighted torch carried by relay from the site of the ancient Games in Olympia, Greece. Following a twenty-minute speech by Olympics organizer Dr. Theodor Lewald, Hitler said just a few words — his only public pronouncement during the Games: *"Ich verkünde die Spiele von Berlin zur Feier der elften Olympiade neuer Zeitrechnung als eröffnet."* (I proclaim open the Games of Berlin, celebrating the eleventh Olympiad of the modern era.)

Adolf Hitler, flanked by Dr. Theodor Lewald (*right*) and IOC president Henri de Baillet-Latour, enters the Olympic stadium. *Bundesarchiv Koblenz, Germany.*

AFRICAN AMERICAN SUCCESSES

Two weeks of Olympic athletic competition began on Sunday, August 2. In the men's track and field events scheduled during the first week, ten of the sixty-six men competing for the United States were African Americans. They won eight out of the twelve events won by Americans. The African American athletes at the Berlin Games captured a total of fourteen gold, silver, and bronze medals in individual and team events. Many American journalists hailed the victories of James "Jesse" Owens and other African Americans as a blow to the Nazi myth of "Aryan supremacy."

The hero of the Olympics was Ohio State track star Jesse Owens, who took home four gold medals. Owens won the long jump and the 100-meter and 200-meter sprints and was a member of the winning 4 x 100-meter relay run. Setting a new world record in the 100 meters run in 10.3 seconds, he was called the "fastest human being." But although Owens was the "mainstay" of

In the broad (long) jump Owens leaped 26 feet 5¹/₂ inches, an Olympic record. Immediately after the Games, hoping to capitalize on his fame, he quit the AAU's European tour of post-Olympic meets; for this action, he was suspended from amateur competition. August 4, 1936. *Bundesarchiv Koblenz, Germany.*

the American team, as stated by one newspaper with a large African American audience, the *Chicago Defender,* he was "not the whole show. Where he leaves off other Americans, and interestingly enough Americans of his race, take up."

Other African American medal winners were Marquette University graduate Ralph Metcalfe, who trailed Owens by only one-tenth of a second in the 100 meters after a slow start. California college student Cornelius Johnson and Ohio State graduate David Albritton finished first and second in the high jump. University of Oregon graduate Matthew "Mack" Robinson, whose younger brother

Matthew "Mack" Robinson (1914–) was born in Cairo, Georgia, to a poor sharecropper family. In the 1920s he moved with his mother and four sisters and brothers to California. Robinson led the Pasadena Junior College track team to become Southern California Champion in 1936 by winning in the broad jump, low hurdles, and sprints. After the Olympics, where he took second place to Owens in the 200-meter sprint, Robinson competed for the University of Oregon track team and became NCAA champion in the 220-yard and 200-meter races and the long jump. Commenting later on the reception given African American athletes in Nazi Germany, Robinson said, "There at least we didn't have to sit in the back seat of the bus." *Mack and Delano Robinson.*

John Woodruff (1915–) was born in Connellsville, Pennsylvania, the eleventh of twelve children in a poor family. He was the only one in his family to complete high school. Setting national records in the 400-meter, 800-meter, and 1,500-meter runs during his high school years, Woodruff received an athletic scholarship from the University of Pittsburgh. The summer after his freshman year he qualified in the 800-meter run for the Olympics, an event he had never thought about until his coach approached him and asked him to try out for the team. The voyage to Europe for the Games was a great adventure, as Woodruff had never before traveled farther than the fifty miles from his home to Pittsburgh. Upon his return, Woodruff was not allowed to compete in a meet at the Naval Academy in Annapolis, Maryland, because he was black. He later said, "Now, here I'm an Olympic champion, and they told the coach that I couldn't run. I had to stay home because of discrimination. That let me know just what the situation was. Things hadn't changed." *FPG International, New York, N.Y.*

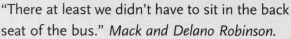

Jackie became the first African American major league baseball player in 1947, took the silver in the 200-meter dash. University of Pittsburgh freshman John Woodruff won the 800-meter run. Archie Williams, from the University of California, Berkeley, won the 400-meter race, and James LuValle, from UCLA, took third in that event. Frederick "Fritz" Pollard from the University of North Dakota captured the bronze medal in the 110-meter hurdles, and in bantamweight boxing, Jack Wilson won the silver.

The African American athletes left Germany with good mem-

The U.S. high jump team swept their event at the Olympics, August 2, 1936. *From left to right:* Delos Thurber (bronze), Cornelius Johnson (gold), and David Albritton (silver). *UPI/Corbis-Bettmann, New York, N.Y.*

ories of their treatment by the German public and the friendships they developed at the stadium and the Olympic Village with athletes from other countries. Owens was pursued everywhere he went and cheered loudly by the largely German audience every time he entered the Olympic stadium. Some African American athletes were invited to German homes for coffee or dinner.

The reception that Owens and other African American athletes received from Nazi leaders was less warm. Both the mainstream and African American press reported that Hitler refused to shake

Posing for a souvenir snapshot, August 1936. *From left to right*: James Clark, middleweight boxer; David Albritton, high jumper; Herb Fleming, a friend; Cornelius Johnson, high jumper; Archie Williams, 400-meter runner; and Fritz Pollard, 110-meter hurdler. *Frank Driggs Collection.*

Jesse Owens's hand or congratulate other African American medalists. In fact, Olympic officers in charge of protocol had urged Hitler to receive all the medal winners or none, and after the first day's events, he chose the latter. Whether he did this to avoid shaking hands with "non-Aryans" is unclear. The Nazi leader could not have been pleased with the bad publicity, as his regime did everything possible to avoid any incidents that would tarnish the image of Germany as the Olympics host. Despite Owens's popularity with the spectators, Hitler never posed for photographs with him as he had done with the blonde Sonja Henie during the winter Olympics.

Nazi censorship of the press prevented German reporters from expressing their opinions freely. A directive to the press of August 3, 1936, stated, "The racial point of view should not be used in any way in reporting sports results; above all Negroes should not be insensitively reported. . . . Negroes are American citizens and must be treated with respect as Americans." Still, one Nazi newspaper demeaned the African American athletes by referring to

Archie Williams (1915–1993) was born in Oakland, California, the oldest of three children. During his sophomore year at the University of California at Berkeley, Williams set a world record in the 400-meter run at an NCAA meet in Chicago. After winning the gold in the event at Berlin and returning home, Williams was forced to stop running because of an injury. Graduating from the University of California in 1939 with a degree in mechanical engineering, he worked during World War II at the Tuskegee Institute in Alabama, a training ground for black pilots. Williams served in the air force for twenty-two years and later taught math and computer science in the San Francisco area high schools for two decades.

Cornelius Johnson (1913–1946) was born in Los Angeles, California. While still in high school, at the age of eighteen, he earned a spot on the track team for the 1932 Los Angeles Games. He placed fourth in the high jump. At the 1936 Berlin Olympics, Johnson breezed through the event, not even removing his sweatsuit until the bar was raised to more than 6 feet 6 inches. Johnson just beat teammate David Albritton. His was the first gold medal won by an American athlete at the Berlin Games.

David Albritton (1913–1994) was born in Danville, Alabama, and at the age of seven moved to Cleveland, Ohio, with his older brother and sister, who raised him after his parents' deaths. A close friend of Jesse Owens, Albritton was a junior at Ohio State University when he qualified for the Olympic track and field team in July 1936. On the first day of events at the Berlin Games, Albritton won the silver in the high jump after a jump-off to break a three-way tie. After his return to the United States, Albritton earned his bachelor's and master's degrees and continued to compete. He worked as a track coach at Alabama State College for several years and later served two terms in the Ohio state legislature.

them as "auxiliaries"—reserve forces without which "one would have regarded the Yankees as the biggest disappointment of the Games." Minister of Propaganda Joseph Goebbels was forced to publicly scold the paper for this statement, although he himself wrote in his private diary after the second day of competition, "We Germans won a gold medal, the Americans three, of which two

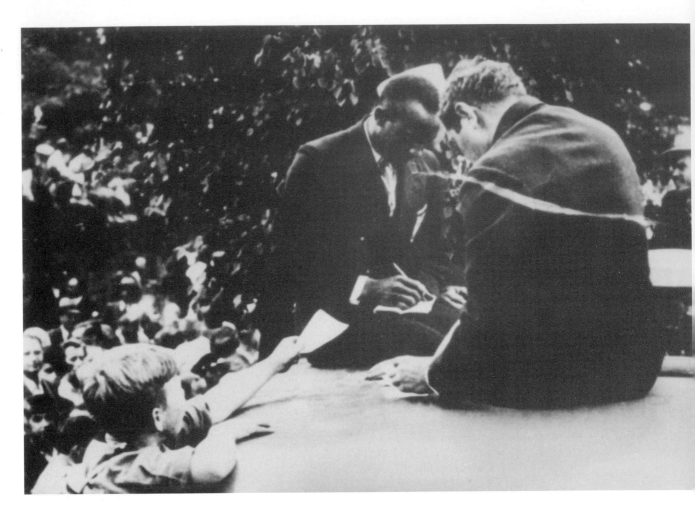

Throughout his stay in Germany, Owens was besieged by autograph seekers. The mostly German audience cheered loudly ("O-VENS! O-VENS!") every time he entered the stadium. July 31, 1936. *UPI/Corbis-Bettmann, New York, N.Y.*

The American press reported widely on the friendship that developed between Owens and his German competitor in the long jump, Carl Ludwig ("Lutz") Long. Long was killed in action during World War II. *Dr. George Eisen.*

This cartoon by Willard Mullin appeared in the *New York World Telegram*, August 6, 1936. It shows the tendency in the American press and radio broadcasts that covered the Games to treat Hitler as a comic figure. Owens is shown carrying an oak seedling, which all gold medalists received at the award ceremony.

were Negroes. That is a disgrace. White people should be ashamed of themselves."

Upon returning to the United States as Olympians, the African American athletes still faced social and economic discrimination. Owens was not offered a Hollywood contract, unlike some of the white athletes from the Berlin Games and previous Olympics. Owens earned money as a political campaigner in the 1936 elections, as a nightclub performer, and as a participant in athletic exhibitions that included racing against horses. During World War II, he served briefly as the head of a government effort to promote physical fitness among African Americans. During the war Olympian John Woodruff served in a segregated army unit, and Archie Williams helped train pilots at the segregated army airfield at Tuskegee, Alabama.

JEWISH ATHLETES AND THE GAMES

Bowing to pressure from the International Olympic Committee, the German Olympic Committee invited German Jewish high jumper Gretel Bergmann to compete at pre-Olympic qualifying meets. In June 1936 Bergmann equaled the German women's high jump record of 5 feet 3 inches at a trial meet in Stuttgart, Germany. But despite her abilities, the Germans decided at the last minute not to include her on the Olympic team, even though they used only two of the three spots given to them for the high jump. In doing so, they probably sacrificed a gold medal. Hungarian athlete Ibolya Csák won the women's high jump at Berlin by clearing 5 feet 3 inches.

As a token to satisfy International Olympic Committee members, German sports leaders invited the part Jewish, blonde fencer Helene Mayer to join the German team in Berlin. Mayer had competed for Germany in the two previous Olympics. At Berlin, she

Gretel Bergmann (1914–) returned to Germany in 1935 at the wish of German sports officials to try out for the Olympic team. Despite her first-place jump at Stuttgart in June of 1936, German officials did not include her on the team. In a form letter dated July 16, 1936, Reich Sports Office leader Tschammer und Osten informed her that she had not made the team. Later, she explained her relief: "Had I won the Olympics or had I been allowed to compete, I would have been a loser either way. Had I won that it would have been such an insult against the German psyche. How can a Jew be good enough to win the Olympics? Then I would have had to be afraid for my life. And had I lost I would have been made into a joke."

Helene Mayer (1910–1953) was invited to join the German Olympic team by Reich Sports Office leader Tschammer und Osten in a letter dated September 21, 1935. On the day she sailed for Germany, she told a *New York Times* reporter that she anticipated the reunion with her mother and two brothers more than anything else and that the "Olympic Games were for international sportsmen and women and not for politicians." She also told him she wanted a chance to win back the championship she lost in Los Angeles in 1932. She came in second at the Games, but in 1937, she won the world championship in Paris, defeating Schacherer-Elek. Mayer returned to California after the Olympics. She went back to Germany after the war and married but died soon after of cancer.

claimed a silver medal in women's individual foil. Two-time European champion Ilona Schacherer-Elek, a Hungarian, won the gold medal in women's individual foil, and the bronze went to Ellen Preis, an Austrian. Like Mayer, both Schacherer-Elek and Preis had Jewish fathers.

A number of other Jewish athletes from Europe and the United States competed in the Olympics. Seven American Jewish men went to Berlin. Most of these young athletes had been pressured by Jewish newspapers or organizations to boycott the Games but chose to go to Berlin. Some of them did not fully understand at the time the extent of Nazi persecution of Jews and how it differed from American antisemitism. Samuel Balter reached the gold

Endre Kabos (1906–1944) won the gold medal for Hungary in the individual saber competition and team saber event. The agile left-handed fencer was one of six Jews on the large Hungarian team who won medals. Many Hungarian Jews shared their fellow citizens' passion for sports and viewed participation as a means of social integration. In the 1930s, however, the antisemitic views of the fascist Hungarian government that developed close ties to Hitler's regime also pervaded some fields of sport. Hungarian fencing officials openly disdained Jews, even champion fencers like Kabos. Kabos would become a victim of World War II: in 1944 he was traveling in a tram that was crossing the Margaret Bridge in Budapest at the moment the structure was blown up by the Germans. *Dr. George Eisen.*

A "non-Aryan" in the eyes of the Nazis, Helen Mayer claimed a silver medal in women's individual foil and, like all other medalists for Germany, gave the required Nazi salute on the podium. The film footage of this moment shows Mayer hesitating awkwardly as she gave the salute, August 5, 1936. *UPI/Corbis-Bettmann, New York, N.Y.*

medal–winning U.S. basketball squad from Hollywood's Universal Pictures team. In 1936 the *California Jewish Voice* urged Balter "to act as a spokesman for his brother Jews" and boycott the Games; the paper vigorously opposed his decision to go. Herman Goldberg was a catcher for the U.S. Olympic baseball team in the exhibition event. Goldberg later recalled, "There were five or six Jewish athletes out of the 300-plus on the team, and some of us were considering whether we would boycott. We came to the conclusion that if the entire team would boycott, we would also do so. But we were really American athletes of Jewish religion. It didn't make sense to us to be the only ones to boycott. We were American athletes, selected by the team to represent our country."

In a controversial move, American coaches benched the only two Jewish runners on the American track and field team, Marty Glickman and Sam Stoller. Both had trained for the 4 x 100-meter relay, but on the day before the event, the coaches informed the young men that they would not compete. Twenty-one-year-old Stoller described the incident in the diary he kept while in Berlin as the "most humiliating episode" in his life. The reasons for the change remain unclear. The coaches claimed they needed their fastest runners to win the race and said this was why they chose a team including Jesse Owens and Ralph Metcalfe. At the time,

Marty Glickman (1917–) was born in New York City five years after his parents emigrated from Romania. Glickman was a freshman at Syracuse University when he qualified for the Olympics. Disappointed that he did not compete at Berlin, he felt that he was young and would "be back and win it all" in 1940. After the Olympics, Glickman ran in London as part of a 4 x 100-meter relay team that set a new world record. That fall, he returned to Syracuse, where he starred in football and track. On one occasion, when he was training for a track meet, the director of the New York Athletic Club denied Glickman entry because he was Jewish. During World War II, he served as a marine corps officer in the Pacific theater. After the war, he became a radio and then television broadcaster, covering games for the Jets, Giants, and Knicks.

Sam Stoller (1918–1983) resided in Cincinnati, Ohio, and was a senior at the University of Michigan at the time of the 1936 Olympics. The day he learned he would not be competing on the 4 x 100-meter relay team as expected, Stoller wrote in his diary, "This is the one day in my life that I'll remember to my dying days." Ten days later, he penned, "I've finally regained my composure. The most humiliating episode in my life has worn off enough so that I can once more think, eat and sleep properly." In his diary entries and later comments to the press, Stoller expressed his view that sports politics, not prejudice, were involved in the last-minute change in the relay team lineup. His disappointment was so great that he swore he would never run again. But upon his return, he won the 100-yard dash in the NCAA championship. Like a number of other Olympians, Stoller had a Hollywood screen test; he would appear in thirteen movies.

many observers, including Stoller, Glickman, and other team members, believed that sports "politics" were the real reason. The two other runners named to the relay team, Foy Draper and Frank Wykoff, had trained under Olympic track coach Dean Cromwell at the University of Southern California. Both Stoller and Glickman had beaten Foy Draper in heats, and at least one of them should have run in his place. Later some individuals, including Glickman, came to believe that antisemitism and Avery Brundage's desire

Marty Glickman (*left*) and Sam Stoller train aboard the SS *Manhattan* on their way to Berlin, July 1936. *Marty Glickman.*

The U.S. 4 x 100-meter relay team. Their time of 39.8 seconds set a world record that held for twenty years. *From left to right*: Jesse Owens, Ralph Metcalfe, Foy Draper, and Frank Wykoff. August 9, 1936. *UPI/Corbis-Bettmann, New York, N.Y.*

not to embarrass Hitler by having two Jewish athletes on the winning podium also helped explain the change. Brundage himself publicly called the charge of antisemitism "absurd" in his final report on the 1936 Olympics.

Germany emerged victorious from the XIth Olympiad. Its athletes captured the most medals when all events were counted, and German hospitality and organization won the praises of visitors. Many newspaper accounts echoed Frederick Birchall's report in the *New York Times* that the Games put Germans "back in the fold of nations," and even made them "more human again." Some writers even found reason to hope that the peaceful interlude would last.

Only a few reporters, such as William Shirer, regarded the Berlin glitter as merely hiding a racist, militaristic regime. In his diary he wrote, "I'm afraid the Nazis have succeeded with their propaganda. First, the Nazis have run the Games on a lavish scale never before experienced, and this has appealed to the athletes. Second, the Nazis have put up a very good front for the general visitors, especially the big businessmen." Propaganda efforts continued well after the Olympics with the world release in 1938 of

Avery Brundage summarized his feelings about the 1936 Olympics in the final report to the American Olympic Committee: "The Games of the XIth Olympiad at Berlin, Germany, was the greatest and most glorious athletic festival ever conducted—the most spectacular and colossal of all time. . . . The 1936 Olympic Games were removed from their normal plane and lifted to a dazzling precedent which probably no country can hope to follow." Three months after the Olympics, Brundage was severely criticized in the press for publicly praising Hitler for instilling a newfound confidence in the German people. "We can learn much from Germany," he advised in a German Day speech at Madison Square Garden in New York City. "We, too, if we wish to preserve our institutions, must stamp out Communism. We, too, must take steps to arrest the decline of patriotism." The boycott movement hardened Brundage's beliefs linking Communism and Jews in a left-wing conspiracy. Brundage continued as a leader in the international Olympic movement, serving as IOC president from 1952 to 1972. *University of Illinois Archives, Champaign-Urbana, Ill.*

Helene "Leni" Riefenstahl (1902–) starred in various films in the 1920s and in 1932 directed her first movie, *The Blue Light,* which caught Hitler's attention. In 1933 Hitler asked her to film the Nuremberg Nazi Party rallies. Her brilliant propaganda film *Triumph of the Will* was released in late 1934 and led to her new assignment filming the Berlin Olympics in 1936. After months of editing of about 1,300,000 feet of film shot by sixty cinematographers, *Olympia* was released in two parts. During the war, Riefenstahl worked as a war correspondent in Poland. Because of her Nazi-sponsored career, *Olympia* and other film materials were confiscated after the war, and Riefenstahl was not allowed to work as a filmmaker in Germany. *Ullstein Bilderdienst, Berlin, Germany.*

Olympia, a controversial film documentary of the Games produced by Leni Riefenstahl. The Nazi regime commissioned Riefenstahl to produce the film, which won first prize at the Venice Film Festival in 1938.

After the Olympics, Hitler pressed on with grand plans for German expansion into new territories. These included taking over the

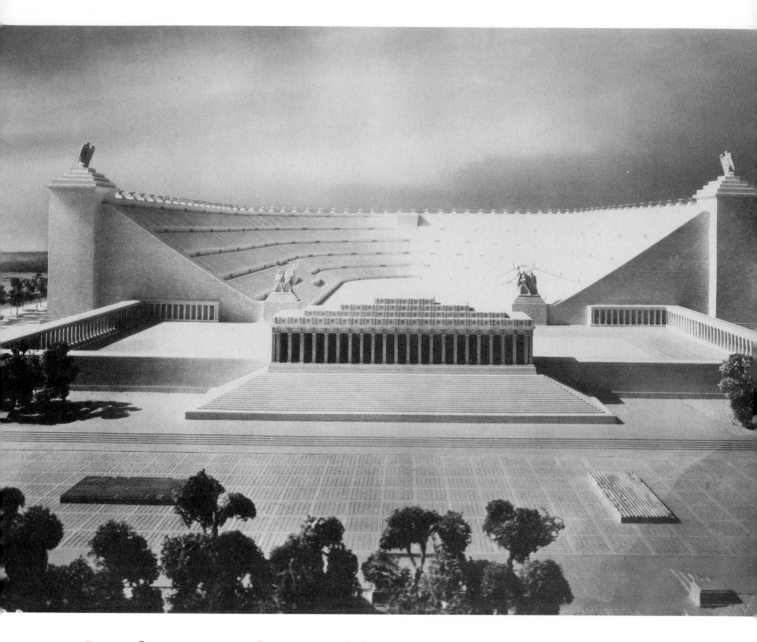

Games forever. In 1937, he inspected designs drawn up by his favorite architect, Albert Speer, for a new stadium at Nuremberg. Speer's model for an enormous four-hundred-thousand-seat stadium greatly pleased Hitler, who loved to use monumental building forms as a way of showing Germany's superiority. When Speer told Hitler that the dimensions of the field did not conform to Olympic standards, Hitler told him not to worry: "In 1940 the Olympic Games will take place in Tokyo. But thereafter they will take place in Germany for all time to come."

Architect Albert Speer's model for a new colossal Olympic stadium. It was never built. *Stadtarchiv Nürnberg, Germany.*

Gretel Bergmann (1914–) obtained papers to emigrate to the United States in 1937. Landing in New York with $10, all the money the Germans allowed her to take out of the country, she found jobs as a masseuse and maid and, later, a physical therapist. She was American national champion in the high jump and shot put in 1937 and the high jump again in 1938. Her mother, father, and two brothers fled to the United States in 1939. Many others in her family, including her grandparents and her husband's parents, were murdered in Nazi camps during the war. In 1996 the German Olympic Committee apologized to the for-mer athlete, inviting her to be their guest at the Atlanta Games. Wanting to end this chap-ter of her life, she accepted.

Captain Wolfgang Fuerstner was a loyal army officer who had directed the German military's athletic program. A few weeks before the foreign Olympic teams arrived in Berlin, Fuerstner was replaced as Olympic Village Commander by Lieutenant-Colonel Werner von zu Gilsa. Fuerst-ner continued to perform his duties as second in command of the Vil-lage through the end of the 1936 Games. Most Jews and part Jews viewed as "non-Aryans" had been removed earlier from the military forces, and Fuerstner's service in overseeing the construction and organization of the highly praised Olympic Village did not save him from the humiliation of dismissal. He shot and killed himself following a banquet held in Gilsa's honor at the close of the Games. Captain Fuerstner was buried with military honors, and the German press ini-tially covered up his suicide, claiming he died from injuries suffered in an automobile accident. *Ullstein Bilderdienst, Berlin, Germany.*

The pause in Germany's anti-Jewish campaign was brief. William E. Dodd, the U.S. ambassador to Germany, had reported that Jews awaited "with fear and trembling" the end of the Olympic truce. Two days after the Olympics ended, Captain Wolf-gang Fuerstner, head of the Olympic Village, killed himself after he was dismissed from active military service because of his Jew-ish ancestry. In 1938 German troops marched into Austria, and the Nazis stepped up the anti-Jewish campaign. On the evening of November 9–10, 1938, *Kristallnacht* (the night of broken glass),

rioters burned more than one thousand synagogues in Germany and in annexed Austria. They vandalized and looted seven thousand Jewish businesses and homes and killed dozens of Jews in an assault organized by Minister of Propaganda Joseph Goebbels. Despair drove many Jews to suicide after *Kristallnacht,* while many more fled the country.

The Eberswalde synagogue in suburban Berlin was one of hundreds of synagogues set afire by anti-Jewish rioters on the night of November 9–10, 1938. *Bildarchiv Abraham Pisarek, Berlin, Germany.*

THE WAR AND THE HOLOCAUST

In March 1939, German troops marched into Czechoslovakia, and five and a half months later, Germany invaded Poland. Within just three years after the Olympics, the welcoming host of the Games had unleashed World War II. In 1940, German and other Axis forces invaded the countries of western Europe — Denmark, Norway, the Netherlands, Belgium, Luxembourg, and France. In 1941, a couple of months after German troops invaded Yugoslavia and Greece, Hitler launched "Operation Barbarossa," a massive attack on the Soviet Union. In 1943 the German army marched into Italy and the following year into Hungary.

During the war, millions of Jewish men, women, and children who lived in the countries of Europe occupied by Germany became the victims of Hitler's "final solution to the Jewish problem." Planned by men at the highest levels of Hitler's government, the "final solution" aimed to destroy all Jews in Europe. Hundreds of thousands of Germans helped carry out the plan, with the assis-

tance of local police, government officials, and others in the occupied countries.

Between 1939 and 1945, up to six million Jews across German-occupied Europe were murdered. More than one million Jews were killed in mass shootings in occupied territories of Poland and the Soviet Union. Nearly three million Jews were deported in trains and trucks from all over Europe to Auschwitz-Birkenau and five other killing centers in occupied Poland. After their arrival at these extermination camps, they were herded into gas chambers disguised as

Hitler and army officers review troops marching inside Poland after the German invasion on September 1, 1939. *USHMM Photo Archives.*

The Dutch gymnastics team won the gold medal at the 1928 Olympics. Five members and the trainer were Jewish. All but one woman were killed in the Holocaust: Estella Agsteribbe (*first row, third from right*), who died in Auschwitz, September 9, 1943, with her husband, Samuel Blitz, and their two children; Helena Nordheim (*first row, second from left*), who died in Sobibór, July 2, 1943, with her husband, Abraham Kloot, and their daughter; Anna Polak, who died in Sobibór, July 23, 1943, with her husband, Barend Dresden, and their daughter; Judikje Simons, who died in Sobibór, March 20, 1943, with her husband, Bernard Themans, and their two children; and their trainer, Gerrit Kleerekoper, who died in Sobibór, July 2, 1943, with his wife, Kaatje Ossendrijver, and their two children. Elka de Levie (*second row, first from right*) survived the Holocaust.

showers and killed. Hundreds of thousands more Jews died from starvation, disease, and brutal treatment in ghettos and concentration camps set up by the Nazis across German-occupied Europe.

During this Holocaust, men and women, young and old, rich

Alfred Flatow (1869–1942) won the individual and team parallel bars competitions for Germany and placed second on the horizontal bar at the 1896 Athens Games. On October 4, 1942, Flatow, at the age of seventy-three, was deported from Berlin to the Theresienstadt concentration camp, forty miles from Prague. He died there two months later, one of the thirty-five thousand Jews who died from starvation while imprisoned at Theresienstadt. *The International Jewish Sports Hall of Fame, Wingate Institute, Netanya, Israel.*

János Garay (1889–1944), a Hungarian Jewish fencer, won bronze and silver medals for individual and team saber events at the 1924 Paris Olympics and a gold medal in team saber at the 1928 Amsterdam Games. He was one of 437,402 Jews deported from Hungary after Germany occupied that country in 1944. Garay died shortly thereafter in the Mauthausen concentration camp in Austria. *The International Jewish Sports Hall of Fame, Wingate Institute, Netanya, Israel.*

Oskar Gerde (1883–1944) won the gold medal in the team saber event at the 1908 London Olympics and the 1912 Stockholm Games. He was deported from Hungary in 1944 and died in the Mauthausen concentration camp. He was one of more than 119,000 prisoners who died in that camp. *The International Jewish Sports Hall of Fame, Wingate Institute, Netanya, Israel.*

Lili Henoch (1889–1942) was a champion shot putter and discus thrower for Germany during the 1920s. She missed the opportunity to become an Olympian in 1924 because Germany, still ostracized after World War I by the Western powers, was not invited to the Paris Games. Henoch, with her sixty-six-year-old mother, was deported to the Riga ghetto in German-occupied Latvia on September 5, 1942. Soon after, they were taken from the ghetto with other inhabitants and killed nearby in an *Einsatzgruppen* mass shooting. *The International Jewish Sports Hall of Fame, Wingate Institute, Netanya, Israel; Lili Henoch.*

Otto Herschmann (1877–194?), an Austrian Jewish swimmer, placed second in the 100-meter freestyle in the 1896 Athens Games. He died in the Izbica transit camp in German-occupied Poland. *The International Jewish Sports Hall of Fame, Wingate Institute, Netanya, Israel.*

Roman Kantor (1912–1943), one of Poland's leading fencers, competed in the team and individual épée events at Berlin. He was arrested in Warsaw in 1942 and deported to Majdanek concentration camp and killing center, where he died in 1943. Kantor was one of approximately three million Polish Jews murdered during the Holocaust. *Sports and Tourism Museum, Warsaw, Poland.*

Janusz Kusocinski (1907–1940) set a world record in the 10,000 meters at the 1932 Los Angeles Games, breaking the Finns' traditional domination of the event. A contusion prevented his participation at the Berlin Games. After the German occupation of Poland, the national hero, aged thirty-three, was executed in the Palmiry Forest on June 21, 1940. Kusocinski was one of tens of thousands of prominent Poles killed as part of a German plan to destroy Poland and enslave the Slavic people. *Sports and Tourism Museum, Warsaw, Poland.*

Attila Petschauer (1904–1943), a Hungarian Jewish fencer, won a silver medal in the individual saber and gold medal in the team saber at the 1928 Amsterdam Games. Four years later, he led the Hungarian team that won the gold medal in team saber at the Los Angeles Games. He was tortured to death by antisemitic Hungarian army officers in a forced labor camp during the war. *The International Jewish Sports Hall of Fame, Wingate Institute, Netanya, Israel.*

Werner Seelenbinder (1904–1944), a German wrestler, finished fourth in the 1936 Olympics competition. Seelenbinder, a Communist staunchly opposed to Nazism, thereby missed the opportunity to mount the winners' podium and defy the Nazis by not giving the "Heil, Hitler!" salute, as he had planned. A member of a Resistance group in Germany, he was arrested in 1942 and later beheaded for treason. *Sportsmuseum Leipzig, Germany.*

Ilja Szrajbman (?–1943), national champion for Poland in the men's 200-meter freestyle, swam for the Polish team in the 1936 Berlin Games. Szrajbman was one of tens of thousands of Jews who died from starvation, brutality, and disease during their imprisonment in the Warsaw ghetto. *Sports and Tourism Museum, Warsaw, Poland.*

Johann Trollmann (1907–1943), a Sinti boxer who was expelled from the German Boxing Federation in 1933, died ten years later in the Nazi concentration camp at Neuengamme, Germany. Trollmann was one of an estimated 220,000 to 500,000 Gypsies (Sinti and Roma) killed in countries across German-occupied Europe, victims of Nazi racism. *Hans Firzlaff.*

and poor, famous and unknown, were killed. Athletes, including participants in the Berlin Games and former Olympians, were not spared. All their medals, trophies, and ribbons awarded for achievements in sports meant nothing to Nazis who aimed to "purify" the "Aryan" race by killing those they saw as inferior or undesirable.

In addition to Jewish victims of the Holocaust, patients in psychiatric hospitals and clinics were also killed as well as hundreds of thousands of Gypsies (Sinti and Roma), victims of Nazi racism. Countless others, including Poles, Soviet prisoners of war, political opponents of Nazi rule, Jehovah's Witnesses, and homosexuals, were executed or died from cruel treatment during imprisonment in Nazi prisons and concentration camps.

AFTERWORD

When most Americans think of the 1936 Olympics today, the accomplishments of Jesse Owens above all usually come to mind. His performance at Berlin was remarkable and would inspire later African American Olympians such as Carl Lewis and Wilma Rudolph. But many people falsely think that by capturing four gold medals in track and field events and becoming the hero of the Olympics, Owens destroyed the Nazi myth that claimed the superiority of an Aryan master race. Believing that Owens's participation in the Olympics had such an effect may help Americans feel good about having gone to Olympics held in Hitler's Germany.

In reality, Owens's performance at Berlin, as splendid as it was, had little impact on Nazi racism, which, as we have seen, continued to grow in strength after 1936 to reach its height in the Holocaust. The medals that Owens and other African American athletes took home from Germany also had little effect on racism in the United States. Southern newspapers covering the Olympics would not even print photographs of Owens. When he and his black teammates returned home, they continued to face discrimination in employment, education, and other areas of American life.

In the 1930s, Americans such as Avery Brundage who supported going to the Olympics in Nazi Germany argued that sports and the Olympic Games were separate from politics. What Hitler's Nazi government did was one thing; what happened in Olympic competition was another. Runners or swimmers or gymnasts should not be denied the chance to do what they loved best. As we have also seen, however, sports were not separate from politics in Nazi Germany. The Nazis took over control of both German sports and the Berlin Games. They prevented some athletes such as the

German Jewish high jumper Gretel Bergmann from doing what she loved best, competing.

Some athletes, most but not all of them Jewish, freely chose not to compete in Berlin or in Olympic trials. Members of the organized boycott movement had educated these young men and women about the ruthless actions of Hitler's regime, persecuting Jews and other minorities as well as opponents of Nazi rule. The names of these athletes will not be found in histories of the Olympics or record books. They earned the fate that Jesse Owens's coach said awaited him if he did not compete for a place on the Olympics team: they were forgotten. But athletes who joined the Olympics boycott, the Herman Neugasses, Milton Greenes, Sammy Luftsprings, and Ruth Langers whose stories have been told here, were also heroes. They deserve a place in history, too.

CHRONOLOGY

Entries pertaining to the Olympics and Nazi Sport are in bold.

May 13, 1931   The International Olympic Committee announces that Berlin will be the site of the 1936 Summer Olympics.

July 30–August 14, 1932   The Olympics take place in Los Angeles, but participation is the lowest since 1906. Catastrophic economic conditions due to the Great Depression limit the number of athletes Germany and other countries can afford to send to distant California.

July 31, 1932   Elections give the Nazi Party 230 seats in the German parliament, making it the largest party in Germany.

January 30, 1933   German president Paul von Hindenburg appoints Adolf Hitler chancellor of Germany. Hitler is leader of the National Socialist German Workers (Nazi) Party.

February 28, 1933   The German parliament suspends the freedoms of speech, assembly, and the press and other basic civil liberties.

March 4, 1933   Franklin D. Roosevelt is inaugurated president of the United States.

March 20, 1933   The SS, Hitler's elite guard, establishes a concentration camp at Dachau, Germany, for political opponents of the regime.

March 23, 1933   The German parliament passes the "Enabling Act," giving Hitler the power to establish a dictatorship.

April 1, 1933   The Nazis organize a nationwide boycott of Jewish-owned businesses in Germany.

April 7, 1933   The Nazi government issues a law excluding Jews and political opponents from government employment and university positions. Similar laws enacted in the following weeks affect Jewish lawyers, doctors, and teachers.

April 25, 1933   The Reich Sports Office directs all German sports and gymnastic organizations to carry out an "Aryans only" policy, excluding Jews from competition.

July 14, 1933   The Nazi government enacts the "Law to Prevent Offspring with Hereditary Defects," which mandates the forced sterilization of certain physically and mentally impaired individuals.

November 20, 1933   The American Amateur Athletic Union calls for a boycott of the Berlin Games.

September 13–25, 1934   The American Olympic Committee sends its president, Avery Brundage, to Germany to inspect treatment of Germany's Jewish athletes. Upon returning, Brundage states that German Jewish athletes are being treated fairly and that the Games should go on.

September 26, 1934   The American Olympic Committee votes unanimously to send a U.S. team to the Berlin Olympics.

March 16, 1935   The Nazi government introduces military conscription.

September 15, 1935   The Nazi government decrees the "Nuremberg Laws," racial laws that make Jews second-class citizens and prohibit sexual relations and marriage between Jews and "persons of German or related blood."

October 18, 1935   The American Federation of Labor and the National Association for the Advancement of Colored People officially support a boycott of the Games.

December 6–8, 1935   The American Amateur Athletic Union votes to participate in the Olympics by a vote of 58.25 to 55.75.

February 6–16, 1936   Athletes from countries around the world participate in the Winter Olympics at Garmisch-Partenkirchen, Germany.

March 7, 1936   German troops march unopposed into the Rhineland.

June 19, 1936   Joe Louis is knocked out in a fight against the German boxer Max Schmeling in New York City. Hitler's regime hails the event as a victory for Germany.

July 12, 1936   Prisoners and civilian workers begin construction of the concentration camp Sachsenhausen at Oranienburg near Berlin.

July 16, 1936   In an effort to "clean up" Berlin, police arrest hundreds of Roma (Gypsies) and intern them in the camp at Marzahn in a remote suburb of Berlin.

July 19, 1936   The outbreak of the Spanish Civil War forces the cancellation of a counter-Olympics, "The People's Olympiad," in Barcelona, Spain.

July 30, 1936   The International Olympic Committee votes to oust American Ernest Lee Jahncke, an outspoken supporter of the Olympics boycott, and replace him with Avery Brundage.

August 1–16, 1936   Athletes from forty-nine countries compete in the Summer Olympics in Berlin, Germany.

August 15–16, 1936   To protest the Berlin Olympics, the World Labor Athletic Carnival is held at Randall's Island, New York.

August 18, 1936   Captain Wolfgang Fuerstner, organizer of the Olympic Village in Berlin, commits suicide after his dismissal from active military service by the German government because of his Jewish ancestry.

May 1937   German Jewish track star Gretel Bergmann emigrates to the United States to escape persecution in Germany. In her first year in America, Bergmann wins the high jump and shot put championships.

March 12–13, 1938   German troops invade Austria, and Germany incorporates Austria into the Reich in what is called the *Anschluss* (annexation).

June 22, 1938   Joe Louis defeats Max Schmeling in one round in New York City.

October 1–10, 1938   German troops occupy the Sudetenland in Czechoslovakia.

November 9–10, 1938   In a nationwide pogrom, organized violence against Jews, called *Kristallnacht* (the night of broken glass), Nazis and their collaborators burn synagogues, loot Jewish homes and businesses, and kill at least ninety-one Jews. German police arrest thirty thousand Jews and imprison them in the Dachau, Buchenwald, and Sachsenhausen concentration camps.

March 15, 1939   German troops march into Czech lands and establish the "Protectorate of Bohemia and Moravia."

June 1939 The International Olympic Committee again names Garmisch-Partenkirchen, Germany, to host the Winter Olympics in 1940.

September 1, 1939   German forces invade Poland; World War II begins.

October 1939   Hitler authorizes the beginning of the secret "euthanasia" program. Health-care professionals send many mentally and physically disabled persons to various killing centers in the German Reich where doctors, nurses, and administrative personnel kill them by lethal injection or in gas chambers.

November 1939 Germany withdraws its invitation to host the 1940 Winter Games.

1940 The International Olympic Committee cancels the Olympic Games because of the war.

April 9, 1940   German troops invade Denmark and Norway.

May 10, 1940   German troops invade the Netherlands, Belgium, Luxembourg, and France.

April 6, 1941   German and other Axis forces (Italy, Bulgaria, and Hungary) invade Yugoslavia and Greece.

June 22, 1941   German and other Axis forces invade the Soviet Union in "Operation Barbarossa." German mobile killing squads called *Einsatzgruppen* are assigned to identify, concentrate, and kill Jews behind the front lines. By the spring of 1943, the *Einsatzgruppen* have killed more than a million Jews and tens of thousands of Roma (Gypsies), Communist officials, and members of the Resistance who fought the German occupation forces using hit-and-run guerrilla tactics.

December 7–8, 1941   Japan bombs Pearl Harbor, Hawaii. The next morning, the United States declares war on Japan.

December 8, 1941   Gassing operations begin at Chelmno, a Nazi killing center situated in Polish territory annexed by Germany. At least 150,000 Jews and 5,000 Roma (Gypsies) are killed at Chelmno by August 1944.

December 11, 1941   Germany and Italy declare war on the United States.

January 20, 1942   Senior Nazi officials meet at a villa in the Wannsee section of Berlin to discuss and coordinate the implementation of the "final solution to the Jewish problem."

Spring 1942   Mass gassings begin at the Sobibór, Belzec, and Treblinka killing centers in occupied Poland. A total of 1.5 million Jews are killed by late 1943.

May 4, 1942   SS officials perform the first selection of victims for gassing at the Auschwitz-Birkenau killing center outside the city of Oswiecim in Polish territory annexed by Germany. By January 1945, approximately 1.1 million people are killed in the Auschwitz-Birkenau camp complex; 90 percent of them are Jewish.

1944 The International Olympic Committee cancels the Olympic Games because of the war.

March 19, 1944   German military units occupy Hungary.

May 7–8, 1945   German forces surrender, and the war in Europe ends.

APPENDIX 1: SUMMER OLYMPICS, 1896-1936

Date	Place	Number of Countries	Number of Events	Number of Athletes
April 6–April 15, 1896	Athens, Greece	14	43	245
May 20–October 28, 1900	Paris, France	26	87	1,225
July 1–November 23, 1904	St. Louis, U.S.A.	13	94	687
April 22–May 2, 1906	Athens, Greece*	20	78	884
April 27–October 31, 1908	London, England	22	109	2,035
May 5–July 22, 1912	Stockholm, Sweden	28	102	2,547
1916	Berlin, Germany	canceled— World War I	——	——
April 20–September 12, 1920	Antwerp, Belgium	29	154	2,669
May 4–July 27, 1924	Paris, France	44	126	3,092
May 17–August 12, 1928	Amsterdam, the Netherlands	46	109	3,014
July 30–August 14, 1932	Los Angeles, U.S.A.	37	116	1,408
August 1–August 16, 1936	Berlin, Germany	49	129	4,066

Source: David Wallechinsky, *The Complete Book of the Summer Olympics* (Boston: Little, Brown and Company, 1996).
* These "interim" Games are not counted in Olympic records.

APPENDIX 2: 1936 SUMMER OLYMPICS PARTICIPATING TEAMS

Afghanistan	Costa Rica	Italy	Poland
Argentina	Czechoslovakia	Japan	Portugal
Australia	Denmark	Latvia	Romania
Austria	Egypt	Liechtenstein	South Africa
Belgium	Estonia	Luxembourg	Sweden
Bermuda	Finland	Malta	Switzerland
Bolivia	France	Mexico	Turkey
Brazil	Germany	Monaco	United States
Bulgaria	Great Britain	The Netherlands	Uruguay
Canada	Greece	New Zealand	Yugoslavia
Chile	Hungary	Norway	
China	Iceland	Peru	
Colombia	India	The Philippines	

Source: Cigaretten-Bilderdienst GmbH, *Die Olympischen Spiele 1936 in Berlin und Garmish-Partenkirchen* (Hamburg-Bahrenfeld, 1936).

SUGGESTIONS FOR FURTHER READING

The 1936 Olympics

Baker, William J. *Jesse Owens: An American Life*. New York: Free Press, 1986.

Constable, George. *XI Olympiad*. Los Angeles: World Sport Research and Publications, Inc., 1996.

Eisen, George. "Voices of Sanity: American Diplomatic Reports from the 1936 Berlin Olympiad." *Journal of Sport History* 11, no. 3 (winter 1984): 56–78.

Glickman, Marty (with Stan Isaacs). *The Fastest Kid on the Block*. Syracuse, N.Y.: Syracuse University Press, 1996.

Guttmann, Allen. *The Games Must Go On: Avery Brundage and the Olympic Movement*. New York: Columbia University Press, 1984.

———. *The Olympics: A History of the Modern Games*. Urbana, Ill.: University of Illinois Press, 1992.

Levine, Peter. *Ellis Island to Ebbetts Field: Sport and the American Jewish Experience*. New York: Oxford University Press, 1992.

Lipstadt, Deborah. *Beyond Belief: The American Press and the Coming of the Holocaust 1933–1945*. New York: Free Press, 1986.

Mandel, Richard. *The Nazi Olympics*. Urbana, Ill.: University of Illinois Press, 1987.

Wiggins, David K. "The 1936 Olympic Games in Berlin: The Response of America's Black Press." *Research Quarterly for Exercise and Sport* 54, no. 3 (1983): 278–292.

The Holocaust and Nazi Germany

Bachrach, Susan D. *Tell Them We Remember: The Story of the Holocaust*. New York: Little, Brown and Company, 1994.

Bauer, Yehuda, and Nili Keren. *A History of the Holocaust*. New York: Franklin Watts, 1982.

Berenbaum, Michael. *The World Must Know: The History of the Holocaust as Told in the United States Holocaust Memorial Museum*. New York: Little, Brown and Company, 1993.

Spielvogel, Jackson J. *Hitler and Nazi Germany: A History*. New Jersey: Prentice-Hall, 1996.

Yahil, Leni. *The Holocaust: The Fate of European Jewry*. New York: Oxford University Press, 1990.

INDEX

Deutsche Sportjugend
Nürnberg, März 1937

The cover illustration of a Nazi sports magazine (*Deutsche Sportjugend*) portrays the German national soccer team giving the Nazi salute. *John Loaring.*

"Youth Serve the Fuehrer" is the title of this Hitler Youth recruitment poster. This organization mobilized boys into the National Socialist Party community through sport and hiking and later prepared them for combat in war. *Bundesarchiv Koblenz, Germany.*

This poster promotes a special "day of sport" in September 1934 for the Nazi League of German Girls (*Bund Deutscher Maedel*). The BDM was part of the Hitler Youth and aimed to prepare German girls for the future under the motto "*Kinder, Kueche, Kirche*" (children, kitchen, church). *Staatliche Museen zu Berlin, Kunstbibliothek, Berlin, Germany.*

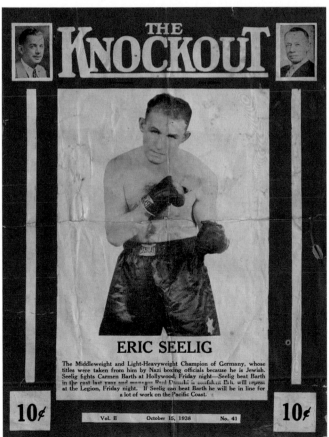

THE
KNOCKOUT

ERIC SEELIG

The Middleweight and Light-Heavyweight Champion of Germany, whose titles were taken from him by Nazi boxing officials because he is Jewish. Seelig fights Carmen Barth at Hollywood, Friday night—Seelig beat Barth in the past last year and manager Paul Damski is confident Eric will repeat at the Legion, Friday night. If Seelig can beat Barth he will be in line for a lot of work on the Pacific Coast.

10¢   Vol. II   October 15, 1938   No. 41   10¢

After the German Boxing Federation expelled amateur boxer Erich Seelig, he resumed his boxing career in the United States. *Mrs. Eric Seelig.*

Professional boxing was among the few racially integrated sports in the United States in 1936, and prizefighter Joe Louis was a hero to African Americans. On June 19, 1936, after rain postponed the fight a day, the undefeated Louis was knocked out by Germany's Max Schmeling. Nazis hailed Schmeling's victory as a triumph for the "new Germany." Schmeling, who was never a Nazi, was warmly received by Hitler after his return to Germany. The fighter was very visible at receptions and other events associated with the 1936 Olympics. In a 1938 rematch, Louis defeated Schmeling in one round. *Research Center, Howard University, Washington, D.C.*

To protest the Berlin Olympics, the World Labor Athletic Carnival was held at Randall's Island, New York, on August 15 and 16, 1936. It was sponsored by the Metropolitan Association of the American Amateur Athletic Union and the Jewish Labor Committee. *Jewish Labor Committee Collection. Robert F. Wagner Labor Archives. New York University, New York.*

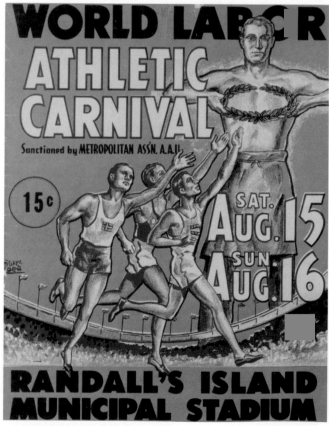

This photomontage entitled "Come and See Germany" was drawn by the German artist John Heartfield (1891–1968) for the July 1936 issue of *Arbeiter Illustrierte Zeitung* (The Worker Illustrated Newspaper), published by German Socialists and Communists in exile. German Minister of Propaganda Joseph Goebbels is portrayed in the foreground holding the Nazi flag. The inscription along the bottom reads: "The purpose of it all: 'Olympic guests: Forward, march!'" *The Heartfield Community of Heirs, © 1996 Artists Rights Society, VG Bild-Kunst.*

The official poster for the 1936 Winter Games at Garmisch-Partenkirchen. *John Loaring.*

The official poster for the 1936 Summer Games at Berlin was created by Nazi artist Franz Wuerbel. It shows an Olympian rising above Berlin's landmark Brandenburg Gate. *John Loaring.*

FACKELSTAFFELLAUF OLYMPIA-BERLIN

A map displays the route of the torch relay from the site of the ancient Olympics in Olympia, Greece, to Berlin. The 1936 Games were the first to employ the torch run. *University of Illinois Archives, Champaign-Urbana, Ill.*

V. OLYMPISCHE WINTERSPIELE GARMISCH-PARTENKIRCHEN 2–11. FEBRUAR 1940

After plans to hold the 1940 Winter Games in St. Moritz, Switzerland, collapsed, Hitler gained an unexpected opportunity to return the Olympics to Germany. In June 1939, Garmisch-Partenkirchen was again named to host the 1940 Winter Olympics. Claiming to have made the decision "regardless of political considerations," the International Olympic Committee voted unanimously to return to Germany "in the interests of sport and the Olympic movement." Germany withdrew their invitation for the Games in November 1939, two months after its forces invaded Poland, marking the beginning of World War II. *Collection of Charles Gary Allison.*

This watercolor portrait of one of Germany's first Olympians, gymnast Gustav Felix Flatow (1875–1945) was painted on sheet music (the only available paper) in the Theresienstadt concentration camp three weeks before Flatow's death from starvation in January 1945. Flatow had been on the German team that placed first in the parallel bars and horizontal bar team events at the 1896 Athens Olympics. After Germany invaded the Netherlands in 1940, Flatow, who had fled there earlier, was arrested. He was later deported from the Westerbork transit camp in the Netherlands to Theresienstadt near Prague, Czechoslovakia, on February 26, 1944. *Forum für Sportgeschichte — Förderverein für das Sportmuseum Berlin, Collection of Stefan Flatow.*